Fetching Dylan

A True Tale of Canine Domestication
in Leaps and Bounds

STEPHEN FOSTER

A PERIGEE BOOK

A PERIGEE BOOK
Published by the Penguin Group
Penguin Group (USA) Inc.
375 Hudson Street, New York, New York 10014, USA
Penguin Group (Canada), 90 Eglinton Avenue East, Suite 700, Toronto, Ontario M4P 2Y3,
Canada (a division of Pearson Penguin Canada Inc.)
Penguin Books Ltd., 80 Strand, London WC2R 0RL, England
Penguin Group Ireland, 25 St. Stephen's Green, Dublin 2, Ireland
(a division of Penguin Books Ltd.)
Penguin Group (Australia), 250 Camberwell Road, Camberwell, Victoria 3124, Australia
(a division of Pearson Australia Group Pty. Ltd.)
Penguin Books India Pvt. Ltd., 11 Community Centre, Panchsheel Park, New Delhi—110 017,
India
Penguin Group (NZ), 67 Apollo Drive, Rosedale, North Shore 0632, New Zealand
(a division of Pearson New Zealand Ltd.)
Penguin Books (South Africa) (Pty.) Ltd., 24 Sturdee Avenue, Rosebank, Johannesburg 2196,
South Africa

Penguin Books Ltd., Registered Offices: 80 Strand, London WC2R 0RL, England

While the author has made every effort to provide accurate telephone numbers and Internet ad-
dresses at the time of publication, neither the publisher nor the author assumes any responsibility
for errors, or for changes that occur after publication. Further, the publisher does not have any
control over and does not assume any responsibility for author or third-party websites or their
content.

FETCHING DYLAN

First American edition: June 2009
Originally published as *Along Came Dylan* in Great Britain by Short Books in 2008.

Perigee trade paperback ISBN: 978-0-399-53511-6

PRINTED IN THE UNITED STATES OF AMERICA

10   9   8   7   6   5   4   3   2   1

This book describes the real experiences of real people. The author has disguised the identities
of some, and in some instances created composite characters, but none of these changes has af-
fected the truthfulness and accuracy of his story.

Most Perigee books are available at special quantity discounts for bulk purchases for sales pro-
motions, premiums, fund-raising, or educational use. Special books, or book excerpts, can also
be created to fit specific needs. For details, write: Special Markets, Penguin Group (USA) Inc.,
375 Hudson Street, New York, New York 10014.

0 1021 0241767 6

For T.A., once more, with love

The Silver Grizzle
Leaves Home

D'you know what, I think he's thrown a litter of smooths!" says the breeder Karen, as she rearranges half a dozen two-week-old pups, maneuvering each of them into the optimum feeding position. Every time she moves one she looks closely at its minute ears to see if there's any sign of the feathering that distinguishes the ears of their mother, Tareefa. It seems there is not. Tareefa is behaving impeccably, lying on her side, quietly sanguine, while six mouths work away ferociously at her nipples. I've never seen pups this young at their feed before. They are no bigger than gerbils, their eyes are closed, and the only way they express personality is by being the hungriest. This is a keenly fought event, in which the competition is intense, and a winner is difficult to find, though the shy one is easy to spot.

By "he" Karen means the proud father, Farid. It was the sight of Farid with his beautiful gray coat and his unfeathered, *smooth* ears, and his relaxed and thoughtful attitude to go with the good looks, that inspired me to pursue an idea. The idea was one I'd been worrying at for a while. The idea was to get a second dog.

I'd had it in my mind for some time that, since Ollie (the subject of my previous book, *Walking Ollie*) had become more or less normal, what he really needed—to encourage and promote the normality—was a companion. Because I could already see him backsliding. Where, pre-normality, he used to be vaguely psychotic, post-normality he was beginning to show signs of going the other way, of becoming moody and withdrawn. I was not principally looking for a new dog for us; I was looking for a perk-me-up friend and companion for him.

It is not as straightforward as all that, though.

When Trezza, my partner, and I discovered Ollie in a rescue shelter five years ago, I knew nothing about dogs. While I am still no expert, I am more experienced than I was then. The long and short of *Walking Ollie* is that Ollie was a very awkward animal, one that I often wished could be sent back whence he came. However (the big however), I could never find it in me to load him into the car, turn the key, and drive him off in order to return him as if he were a faulty television. Dogs are not like that. Dogs get under your skin. After you have cared for one for a while (and you do have to care for them, they are not into looking after themselves), you find that, quite unconsciously, you have become absorbed into a cult: the Cult of the Dog Owner. In this way, it has to be conceded, you, too, have become slightly cultish— which is surely another word for crazy—just like all the rest of them.

This is how, and why, you begin to think along these lines, the lines along which I had been thinking. Even without Ollie's incipient personality change into "the loner," it had been crossing my mind that, since he no longer runs away when he catches sight of me, since he sometimes responds to the call of his name, since he is less fearful of plastic bags and flies than he used to be, what must happen next is a matter of inevitability.

Each time the thought appeared, I pushed it away

because it was a thought that would, in all probability, make life much more difficult than it needed to be. Keeping two dogs will not be any less trouble than keeping one, will it? And it's unlikely that it will turn out to be just double the trouble, either. No, without pausing to recollect those incidents you have witnessed, or been part of, or have started—incidents involving a pair of dogs simultaneously going missing in opposite directions—without bothering to recall moments of that sort, it's still easy enough to guess that two dogs will be trouble multiplied and squared.

But (the big but, bigger than the big however).

But: I looked at Ollie lying in his basket, bored and fed up, fed up and bored, filled with ennui and actually *sighing*. I looked at him day after day, and the more I looked at him, the more I convinced myself that the cause of his apathy was the lack of a playmate. He has me; he has Trezza; he has Jack, my teenage son, who sometimes comes around; and he has Jack's friends, who also sometimes come around. He is not particularly interested in any of this group of individuals.

At least he sees the great outdoors twice a day, in fields and on beaches and around lakes. Here he has a number of friends (and enemies) to meet and greet (or not). Here he can normally be relied upon to be fairly lively. It is only all the many hours that he spends indoors, like a bored teenager who has *nothing to do*, that seem difficult for him. I can keep putting off the search for a companion for him for as long as this remains the case. The rational part of me is capable of thinking of it in these terms: "Tough shit, Ollie. Here you are in the warm and dry being loved and fed and everything, what a hardship."

It's when he starts to become surly, withdrawn, and lethargic in the great outdoors that I really believe something needs to be done. He has always had these tendencies in the house, as well as many other special characteristics: for instance, there was a time he was frightened of everything, up to and including (most especially) me, his loving master. It was a huge problem, but after many difficult months we got through that. This left only a secondary raft of neurosis, including a fear of aprons and of flies, but the longer time went on, the more he relaxed and the more our relationship really became that of loving master and faithful, albeit disobedient and scatty, companion.

***

I surfed the Internet, looking at the rescue sites. I saw numerous deserving cases, some of which I considered at length, repeatedly revisiting the relevant web page, downloading the picture to my desktop, emailing it on to Trezza's computer downstairs, but in truth I was never going to acquire a companion for Ollie from these sources because here were animals who could turn out to be even more trouble than *he* was. And this matter crossed my mind, too: Ollie might not appreciate a rival in the special-needs stakes. What I was looking for was a pup, someone that Ollie could train into his ways. I did the mental checklist. Which breeds does Ollie most like; who does he play with? There is no definitive answer to this. He is selective; he has one Doberman he loves, a couple of terriers that he is always delighted to see, a pair of mutts that he rates highly, and a continental sparring partner, an Italian Spinone (an engaging animal, but one that is the embodiment of the Who album title *Meaty Beaty Big and Bouncy*). So: not an Italian Spinone, in any event.

Ollie is a lurcher, a crossbreed, half Saluki, half greyhound. The greyhounds that we regularly encounter are quiet, retired animals who do very little. Ollie will occasionally have a run with one of these, but only occasionally, because nine times out of ten the greyhounds can't be bothered. It's probable, in fact, that it's his greyhound side that is responsible for the incipient lethargy. I looked around my neighborhood. In a (single sample) proof of this theory I noted that the one greyhound we saw every day was an idler who slouched along behind his master, a curmudgeon who walks with a stoop and who is never without a cigarette that he spends most of his life relighting.

To the best of my knowledge we had never, on any of our walks, met the other side of Ollie, a pure Saluki. Salukis are of Bedouin origin and are somewhat greyhound-like to look at, but they differ considerably in temperament: people tell me that Bedouin tribesmen have two words for canines, one is *dog*, the other is *Saluki*. So far as Bedouin tribesmen are concerned, the Saluki is in some way distinct from the rest of its kind.

One way in which Salukis are distinct is that they are high maintenance, in the way that supermodels are high maintenance: the price to be paid for their aesthetic beauty comes in ludicrous demands and self-centeredness. But though everything must be five-star in their world, they are not remotely fastidious: they will, as we shall discover, put more or less anything into their bodies, and they are martyrs to their unpredictable temperaments.

Though we have met no pure-bred Salukis, Ollie has frequently bumped into his fellow travelers from the world of Saluki-crosses. These almost always originate from a rescue shelter, like Ollie himself. Without this source of supply, and short of breeding your own, I don't know where you'd find one. Gypsies and travelers use and abuse them for poaching: that is how so many of them end up in shelters. It was this "poacher-abandoned" category that was responsible for throwing up so many of the deserving cases that I had been looking at online. Ollie's view of his fellow Saluki-crosses is that he likes them more than most. They have a way of playing that is all their own, one that begins with bouncing on the hind legs combined with a zigzag scissor-action and much standing-off and shadow-boxing before anything actually happens. It's a kind of canine tai chi on fast-forward.

So. I put two and two together, come up with five, and switch my search to Saluki websites.

It is here that I see the picture of Farid. I send a link to Trezza's computer. The picture of Farid is of a pose in which his legs are splayed forward and his backside is stuck up in the air, a position that Ollie goes into in moments of joy or happiness, or sometimes for no reason at all. Trezza comes up to my office in a flash. My word, she says, he looks a nice boy, doesn't he?

"Are there any plans for this Farid to become a dad?" I ask the website via email.

A day or two later the reply bounces back. "There may be."

They're a cagey lot, breeders, particularly of the more marginal dog types. "Who's asking?" That's the first thing they want to know. "Are you thinking of getting into the breed and winning certificates in shows, *certificates that belong to me? Or, worse, are you an agent for a rival, some scoundrel who is *already* in the breed and who is trying to pull a fast one?"

That's what they're thinking. Or at least, that's what I think they're thinking.

***

We drive a hundred miles to where Farid lives, to meet him and Karen. I go along wearing my most innocent demeanor: I am just a regular guy looking for a pup, that's all. We are greeted warmly, with a complete absence of any of the suspicions that I have invented. There are five or six Salukis at the house, and really, it is they who interview us. "Are you people fit to own a dog from our noble lineage?" This is what their expressions say. If they were feline, rather than canine, they would be the Aristocats. At some point during this interview, Farid climbs up and sits next to Trezza on a sofa. While we are drinking tea and nibbling on smoked salmon sandwiches and talking with Karen, Farid secretly removes the scrunchy from Trezza's hair using the "stealthy teeth" method. We are won over. A couple of weeks later we return, this time with Ollie accompanying us. The plan is for Farid and Ollie to go out for a walk. I feel I have to apply this test, because, though he generally likes other running dogs, there *are* exceptions, and I want to make sure that Farid is not one of these. He is not. In fact, Ollie bosses him around a bit, which is perfect; I want him to be slightly dominant: I can't have a kid coming into the house and usurping him, because that would have catastrophic consequences for the delicate Ollie psyche. Now, I feel that I have carried out as many safeguards as I can think of without applying a proper measure of common sense and abandoning the idea altogether.

"Yes," I say on the phone a few days later. "Yes: we would like a pup from the noble lineage of Farid."

So here we are . . . leaning over the whelping box, looking at the litter of six, wondering which one to choose. Half the decision is made for us: three are bitches, and they are already spoken for. Of the dogs, two are a more traditional black with cream highlights (similar to Doberman markings); the remaining one is a gray like Farid.

He is a "silver grizzle," says Karen, giving me the technical term.

He is a greedy little silver grizzle, too; he is going for the Suckler of the Week Award, and he is definitely going to win it. He is also the one we fancy. Can we have him?

As it turns out, we can. The bitches are all black and cream, too. Our boy is the exceptional one, colorwise. I feel quite elated. Trust me, breeders have it all planned out in advance, and I can only assume that it is because we were on the scene so early—before Farid had even got intimate with Tareefa—that we have been honored by being allowed to purchase, for a healthy fee, the dog that we actually want.

We make a return to see "Ghali" (his "kennel name"),

who we have by now decided will be known as Dylan (I *cannot* stand in the park shouting, "Ghali! Come here you little sod!"). We have named him after Bob. This will turn out to be a prescient and appropriate choice when we hear his wide range, and variety, of tuneless singing. The litter are six-week-olds at this penultimate visit. I sit on the floor of Karen's kitchen while each of them comes along to bite my fingers and let out a little warm piss into my lap, so that they can remember where I am, for next time. Their teeth are like needles; I note that Tareefa will pick any of them up in her mouth and launch them out of the way if their suckling becomes too enthusiastic. You can hardly blame her. I note also that Dylan's belly is covered in pinprick marks from sibling teeth, as well as a plentiful number of scratches (as indeed are all of their bellies). They are certainly keen on a bit of rough and tumble. This can only stand him in good stead for the future.

We visit Karen for the final time. They are twelve weeks now. Dylan has been washed and shampooed. He looks and smells lovely as he sits on a towel on the kitchen floor waiting; for what, he cannot know. His siblings are behind a wrought-iron gate in the utility room, some asleep, some keeping watch. Dylan trembles slightly and looks very lost and lonely. He is the first one to be separated, and for a moment I think it's cruel, that we should just leave him there to live with his family. But then I have the counter thoughts: this is a family that is going to be broken up imminently in any event, and a pack of dogs left to mature would surely just fight each other all day long until only the pack leader is left alive. We are not being cruel, we are being kind!

Trezza sits Dylan on her lap in the back of our battered station wagon. Karen turns away with a tear in her eye as I wheel the car around and take to the road on the way to introduce the pup to his new life in Norwich. He looks very nervous, and as if to demonstrate that this is not just an act—that, in fact, he really *is* very nervous—he projectile vomits a couple of times somewhere around Thetford Forest.

***

Ollie, who increasingly models himself on Howard Hughes, lives alone in a penthouse flat, in his basket in Trezza's office. He never stirs when the postman rings the bell, or when the door opens, or when visitors arrive. It's no different when his owners return home, and it's no different now.

"Ollie!" we call. "Come see who we've got!"

It's a bit of an imposition, but he manages to tiptoe to the top of the stairs. Dylan is in my arms at the foot of the flight. Ollie pauses. You're joking aren't you, he seems to say, as he turns on his heel and goes back to his bed. He is certainly not going to dignify this unseemly turn of events by coming down for a closer inspection.

"That was your big brother," I say to Dylan. "He's a bit weird."

Dylan as a pup: "I would never pee on this rug very often."

Born to Run

After two solid weeks of Ollie ignoring Dylan (his technique was to stare at the ceiling every time he thought the new arrival might be about to visit his room), I was beginning to become concerned. Ollie is an obdurate individual and I could easily foresee him setting a world record for giving the cold shoulder.

Dylan, meanwhile, had other concerns beyond the elusive presence upstairs. He cried every night for the first week, reinforcing the idea that had crossed my mind about it being cruel to remove him from his brood. Each time he cried I got out of bed and went downstairs to stroke him until he fell back to sleep in his basket next to the radiator in the laundry room. I remembered having to do something like this with Jack when he was a baby, and not for the first time I wondered at those men who start second families in their forties. After the novelty of the regular leg-over with the younger model has faded away, has it ever been known for such an individual to be happy? No. Why? Because getting up to look after a wailing infant four times a night for months on end (and then having to repeat it all over again when the second one comes along) is a young man's game.

Dylan was in the habit of crying early in the morning, too. I propped my eyes open and prepared him his breakfast of porridge made with goat's milk and honey, with the addition of a raw egg every third day (breeder's instructions). I made tea for myself, and after he'd eaten I settled him on my knee on the sofa. Here I discovered that Channel 4 was showing old episodes of *Friends* first thing, and here I discovered what an ideal way that is to start the day. After this there was another American sitcom, new to me, called *Everybody Loves Raymond*; it was okay, but *Friends* was the main event. Dylan began to squirm—we had had enough TV. We left the house for five minutes to go around the corner where there is a patch of grass, to attend to toilet activities, or more likely not: he was loath to go until he really felt that he was *out*, that is out in real nature. Back indoors he might have a little tinkle on a rug, in secret somewhere, and then, to distract me from finding the evidence, demand that we play ball. We did that in the hall until he was tired out, which only took an hour. Once he'd dozed off, I sneaked Ollie downstairs, past Dylan, without waking him, so that *he* could take *his* normal exercise, away at the fields of the university. By the time I was back Dylan was awake, singing noisily to himself, and the feeding and playtime began again. Like a parent (even a young one) with a second new baby, I was beginning to grasp the full horror of what the hell I had done: by the time I had finished dealing with the dogs, I was left with sixty minutes of daylight that I could count as my own free time. You can't get much writing done in an hour, as that is only long enough to make coffee, read the sports pages, and go down to the corner shop to replenish your stock of chocolate cookies.

The reason I did not take them out together (Ollie's attitude aside) was that there was too much of an imbalance in size, which I knew would translate into an inability for them to play fairly together. Beyond this,

Dylan could shoot up and down our hall like a rocket; in an extended version of this skill he was not all that straightforward to control on the leash during those five-minute (non)toilet breaks. I was not yet prepared to take them out as a pair, as I thought this would cause serious handling difficulties.

But Dylan had a great deal of energy to expend, more than indoor ball games could account for. So I began showing him the ropes by walking him alone in a small local woods. The first new dog he met here was a Border collie pup of the exact same age, called Moss. Upon sighting Moss, Dylan ran backward while yapping like a maniac, finally settling himself into a place of safety between my legs, where he sat and trembled. Oh no. I would never have thought of him as a timid creature, not from what I had so far seen of his Speedy Gonzales act in the hall, or from the rest of his demeanor either: whenever we came into the house he was immediately there to see what excitement would happen next, and he took a keen interest in everything we did, especially if it involved the preparation of food; opening the fridge door was enough to wake him from the deepest of sleeps. He was hyperalert to anything in the world that might potentially be comestible, or indeed potable: he went out of his way to follow me to the bathroom, where he stuck his head between my legs from behind and tried to get his nose into my stream of pee. Once or twice I had to rescue him from the depths of the porcelain where, having been left unattended for three seconds, he had taken his opportunity and made it his business to put the contents of the "indoor well" to the taste test.

We had installed a child's stair-gate at the foot of the stairs to prevent him from having the run of the whole house—flights of stairs are not recommended as training grounds for pups. He was making repeated surreptitious attempts, using his paws and teeth, to slip the lock on this stair-gate in an effort to discover what was with this Ollie character, and what was with everything else that went on up on the mysterious second floor, too. When this proved too difficult, he turned his attentions to quietly removing the carpet from the bottom stair in preparation for tunneling under the gate. I knew when this had been going on—like a prisoner walking around the parade yard shaking dirt out of his trouser leg, Dylan would be covertly spitting lumps of Stainmaster into the corner of his basket.

Indoors, in all respects, Dylan was the anti-Ollie; indoors he did not seem the shy type at all.

I tickled this Moss behind his ears. "Look Dylan," I said, "he's a nice boy. He could be your friend."

Dylan replied by staying put and sticking to his trembling.

We met a second dog, an adult Labrador. This time things were different; this time Dylan stood his ground, yapping like a maniac before flirting back to the place of safety between my legs, where he sat and howled like a wolf. It was an extraordinary noise coming from an animal who was so slight that if you sat him on a napkin there would be enough room for another pup beside him. The other owner did her best not to laugh.

I made my diagnosis: he had an excess of nervous energy that needed to be released. I had asked Karen when it was safe to let him run—some breeds aren't allowed full athletic freedom until they are six, seven, or eight months old, because of the detrimental effects it can have on joints and tendons in later life. But Karen had said that she'd always let her dogs loose from the outset, that they are light on their feet and do not develop those kinds of problems. It's good for them to get some proper exercise, she said, but advised *not* to let Dylan go full speed with an adult running dog as, in a worst-case scenario, he might "blow his lungs up."

So, on a path in the middle of the small woods, with no adult running dogs in sight, I let him off the leash.

When I was a boy I had a toy car that you revved by repeatedly rolling the wheels on the floor to crank up the mechanism. When you let it go, it flew off at full speed and crashed into the nearest piece of furniture or the ironing board. This was Dylan, with the addition of a pair of ears that he had not yet grown into, which flapped about as if they belonged to Dumbo the Flying Elephant. Though the ears brought to mind a pair of parachutes, they did not in any way act as brakes. More like wings. He flew up and down the main path and in and out of the adjacent trees and bushes in one single action, a blur. The effect was too much for the other passing owners. They stood and laughed until tears ran down their faces while calling their friends on their cell phones. "Are you near the woods? Come down and check this out," they said. "Be quick."

Once he was good and done with his cartoon caper, a dozen imprecations to come and take treats were all it took to bring him back to my hand. He liked his freedom all right. Back home, after he'd eaten a bowl of food with all the finesse of a hyena, and begged for seconds (pig's ear), he crawled into his basket where he slept the sleep of the righteous; I tiptoed Ollie out past him for *his* exercise and then, finally, I was left with the single free hour of my own time.

This routine could not go on, of course. Even writers have to do something beyond unpaid, self-inflicted, twelve-hours-a-day kennel-husbandry in order to make ends meet.

Teething Troubles

After two weeks of "no thaw" in Ollie's cold-war stance, the time had come to take direct action. I carried Dylan upstairs and advised Ollie that this was his new stepbrother and he'd better get used to it, like it or not. I put Dylan down to see what would happen, to see if he was prepared to make the first move, the step that Ollie would never take. It's not often you see a look of disgust cross a dog's face (because very few things disgust an animal who devotes hours to licking his own private parts), but Ollie treated me to just such an expression now.

Dylan, on the other hand, was delighted to finally make the acquaintance of the recluse. He demonstrated his delight by getting into bed with Ollie, where he offered himself up for a fight by diving into him and play-boxing. Ollie stepped out of his basket wearing another look you don't often see on a dog, one of contempt. He stood and glowered at the interloper. Dylan stepped out of Ollie's basket, bit Ollie on the leg, then bounced back into the (much) bigger dog's bed, expectantly. Ollie looked around to me, for help. "C'mon," he seemed to be saying. "A joke's a joke, now take him away." Dylan bit Ollie's leg and bounced back expectantly once more. Ollie instinctively cuffed him on the ear with his paw. Dylan bit Ollie's leg and bounced back expectantly a third time. Ollie is very tall and very long. He stretched forward, took Dylan's head into his mouth and threw him across the room.

"Oh shit," I said.

And *oh shit* I thought, too. I have seen Ollie dismiss certain of his kind before; these decisions are not usually reversible.

I reached down to see if Dylan was injured. Too late. Dylan had already anticipated my reach, had dodged my hand, and had flown back into Ollie's basket, where he embraced his big old playful lanky hooligan stepbrother. *Do it again,* he seemed to be saying, as if being launched across the room arse-first was the greatest game yet. Ollie growled at him, albeit in a reasonably nice way.

I took Dylan back downstairs while I considered the next best move. He had a great many toys with which to play, scattered around his basket and elsewhere, but of course toys are very boring; it is only the packaging in which they arrive that holds a brief glimmer of interest. Once a cardboard box is destroyed (six seconds), well, that's one straightforward and insignificant task out of the way. What next? The eager pup only has to look around to choose from numerous and varied opportunities to enhance and adapt his environment. These present themselves on every horizon; he is spoiled for options. Even a modest knot in a floorboard can be improved by widening and extending into a proper hole. There's a spray you can purchase called Don't-chew-it-boy! or some such. It's supposed to make soft furnishings and table legs unpleasant to a dog's palate; it's about as effective as covering a cookie jar with a paper doily and expecting that to create an antitheft barrier between a schoolboy and a pound of Double Stuf Oreos.

Fetching Dylan

Dylan was quiet and sly and diligent in his modus of destruction. He had inherited the stealthy teeth from his father, and he was exceptionally excellent with them. As with young children, it's extended passages of silence that ought to signal cause for alarm, and as with young children, you don't notice this at first, because the silence is so welcome that you tend to be enjoying it before it dawns on you: something is afoot, the quietness is a mute alarm. You look in the basket where you last saw him. All he has left behind is his impression in a duvet and some spat-out carpet fibers. Where is he? Is he on his second bed on the sofa where Trezza has set him up with a blanket? No. Is he on his third bed on the other sofa where Trezza has set him up with a fleece? No again. You stand and listen. There is a slight scratching coming from somewhere, like a hamster in a cage. You kneel down. Aha, there he is, under the dining room table, further disguised under a dining room chair. The chair has, or rather had, a raffia seat. Dylan's head is sticking up through the hole where the seat used to be: he is wearing the chair like a collar while all around him is a mass of finely shredded wicker. He knows he has done wrong. You can tell this by the way your appearance is the signal for him to fly back into his basket and sit innocently trembling as if to say: it wasn't me, Officer, I wasn't even there.

You give him a very stern look and issue the very stern words: naughty boy, Dylan.

Five minutes later you check up on him (you feel a bit rotten for having told him off like that). No need to worry, he is perfectly happy. He is engrossed in a new task: he has found one of your shoes and has his muzzle right down inside it as he applies himself to the serious business of eviscerating the insole.

Walks

Ollie is a different creature outdoors. He is no longer a recluse; he is, as it were, normal. He is confident. So we bit the bullet and took them out together. We kept Dylan on one of those long extension leashes, the plan being that they could play a little, within limits. We let Ollie off, the usual routine for him. Here, at last, was the moment Ollie had been waiting for. He dived at Dylan. Some might say he was out to kill him. I would interpret it otherwise: he wanted to see what he was made of. Dogs know who's who in the dog world, and even though Dylan was a pup, Ollie would have ascertained in a moment that Dylan was a runner.

But having Ollie free and Dylan on the long leash was a disastrous idea; while Dylan was wrapping a cord around my legs, Ollie was misbehaving in a concerted way: "Let me at him." It was December, gray and wet. Trezza was opposed to the idea, but in the muddy center circle of a soccer field I let them go together. Ollie's mouth went straight into the back of Dylan's neck. This is normal practice for lurchers and other crossbreeds of the lurcher type; this is the technique they employ to provoke each other into chase. Given the disparity in sizes, though, what we had was a David and Goliath–type situation. Unarmed with a sling, Dylan chose defense as the best form of defense, going to the ground while, in the interests of evasion, simultaneously turning 180 degrees. Ollie went after him; Dylan reversed and went through Ollie's legs. Ollie considered that to be cheating and went after him harder. Dylan tried hurdling his brother from a standing start, didn't quite make it, and was knocked back by the ridge of Ollie's spine. Like a prop forward screwing a wing half's head into the turf, Ollie assisted Dylan into the mud by wrapping his jaw around his throat and bearing down. As I went to rescue

Walks

Dylan, he escaped, like a hare. This gave Ollie a chance to test out his new plaything on cornering. He wasn't too bad, though he did keep losing his footing, slipping, and sliding; he was repeatedly using his chin as an emergency hand brake. The expression "blow his lungs up" flashed into my mind. I went to rescue Dylan once more. This time the instinct was two-way: Dylan had decided that enough was enough and hurtled back to the place of safety between my legs. I clipped him to his leash and gave him a tasty bite of steak for being so brave. At this turn of events Ollie cantered around the edge of the field with a studied petulance, as if nothing much had happened, and as if to say, "Take note, little squirt: not only did you lose that encounter by three falls and a submission, but furthermore regard the situation as it now stands—*I* am free, while you, on the other hand, are bound in chains."

Dylan stretched to the end of his extension leash as if to say, "Hey, come back here and try that again if you dare."

They were going to be all right together, eventually. This was my guess.

That they would be all right together, eventually, though, was a matter that only the trained eye might

31

We call this tough love, shorty.

discern. Our friends in the dog world are all more or less well-disposed toward Ollie, and so make allowances for, and are intrigued by, his atypical disposition. He is, for example, part of a minority cult of canines: upon being offered a treat, he will frequently drop it to the ground with a look of suspicion, or even disinterest. And sometimes he will walk away from it, leaving it behind for some other animal to eat. It is this last characteristic that puts him in a category of one; the other animals wait behind Ollie in order to Hoover up his rejects. It is with a certain sense of purpose that some owners experiment with the treats that they keep in their pockets until finally, and in triumph, they discover the one that Ollie will take. Nevertheless, these friends regarded him somewhat askance when they saw how he was behaving toward the little brother.

A trek out along the coast had been arranged. We began with six or seven dogs and finished up as a pack of a dozen or so, as we collected a few more along the way. Ollie devoted the whole of this time to dive-bombing Dylan, thereby discarding ten or more assorted other opportunities to pick on someone his own size. Even the most laissez-faire among the group (those who might be expected to say, "They'll sort it out between themselves") agreed that intervention was required. I was forced to tell Ollie to cut it out. Useless: not only do dogs not understand English, but this is not even Ollie's native tongue. Instead, group action was taken, a cordon was set up around Dylan to keep Ollie at bay. Ollie, recognizing the interdiction, took a different path from the rest of us, making his way along a ridge of dune in a sulk.

After the walk we ate lunch at a dog-friendly village pub, one that invites animals in. Ollie remained where he prefers to be, on his rug in the car, while this meal took place, because going into buildings freaks him out. Dylan had no such qualms. Too exhausted from his initiation into gang life even for begging, he sat on my knee at the dining table, where he fell asleep in the upright position. I settled him down on my lap; his huge ears hung on either side of my leg. A procession of ladies came over and coochy-cooed at him. He raised half a sleepy eyebrow to this saccharine attention and smiled wanly. It was an exhibition of cuteness, a talent that would serve him well in the months ahead, when he had grown a little more and had taken up certain dangerous hobbies, like hitching a lift by sinking his teeth into the tail-stump tow-hook of a Doberman, for instance. He needed a measure of charm to get away with that, and to get away with many more of his "extreme danger" lifestyle activities.

Not so long after the early-days beach walk we picked up on new acquaintances, a character named Philip and his dog, Diddley (after Bo, not after squat). Diddley is a Dalmatian. Dylan and Diddley are the same age, and their respective owners found that walking them together was an excellent method of wearing them out. Though they were both young—and so naturally unruly—Diddley is reasonably well behaved, a lot better behaved than Dylan, that's for sure. Dylan goes selectively deaf when there are better things to do, like chasing squirrels up trees for fifteen minutes. Philip has often commented that what Dylan needs is "to know who's boss." Philip has vaguely questioned my skills as a master by implying that a kick on the backside would do Dylan absolutely no harm whatsoever. But then Dylan (finally) comes back and does not receive a kick on the backside. Instead he slides in, burning holes into his pads as he comes to a halt ten yards beyond his intended stopping point. Here he sits, diligently and expectantly, wearing an expression that says, *Sorry, Officer. Sorry I'm late: I only just heard your shouting and whistling and shouting and whistling and SHOUTING, and clapping your hands and everything. I've been very, very busy. You should see the amount of vermin out there. It's a public disgrace. You haven't got a bit of steak on you at all by any chance? I'm famished.*

"I wonder if he knows how cute he looks," Philip says in his heavy Norfolk accent, as he lights another cigarette and shakes his head. "It does help you get away with it, don't it?" he says to Dylan.

"You can't help but laugh at him though, boy, even if he is a pain in the arse," he says to me.

Philip always calls me boy, it's the colloquial expression of greeting around here. After I had known Philip for some time, I was going through the answering machine deleting messages. Seven out of thirteen were from him, and each one began in exactly the same way: "Hello there, boy, that's only me, Philip."

More of Philip and Diddley soon enough.

Meanwhile . . .

Teething Troubles II:
The Eve of Destruction

Philip is right—I should be more of a disciplinarian. I should at least have treated Dylan to some benign version of his recommended kick on the backside when I first caught him sitting on the nice leather sofa—*on the best furniture!* as my parents used to say—secretly softening the cushions with saliva as a prelude to sinking his teeth in and "taking the kill." And I should have treated him to it once more when, having been banished from the best furniture, all of a sudden, there he was again, this time hanging forward and determinedly customizing the edge of the coffee table. I made this table myself, from a piece of sycamore. It is an uneven shape, a slice of tree with a wavy edge. That's not so bad, I thought, after I'd shoved him off, as I examined the hundreds of puncture marks he had contributed to the widest curve on the promontory of the long edge. I can sand it out later when he's finished cutting his teeth, I thought. Or I might just leave it like that—I could regard his input as an artistic "intervention." Those marks are like a child's first drawings, I thought. They merely contribute to the patina of beauty. It helps to see things this way when you have a puppy. A friend came around just before Ollie first arrived. The friend was an experienced dog owner. I was talking to him about plans I had for installing new kitchen cabinets, as well as about the impending arrival. "Leave it until this pup you're getting has grown up," he advised. "For one," he said, "you don't want your new kitchen ruined; and for two, he'll destroy these for you anyway, whether you like it or not."

After examining the coffee table, I left Dylan sleeping in his basket while I went to do some work in my office, which is in the attic. After a while, after longer than he normally sleeps, I noticed the warning sound of quietness. One floor below, i.e., upstairs (it took him no time at all to work out how to slip the lock on that stair-gate), I found him sitting on *our bed* eating my underwear. He looked very content. It's okay, I could do with some new boxers anyway, I thought. On the floor was a pair of socks with the toe-ends removed. I could do with new socks, too, I thought.

I should be more of a disciplinarian, but I am not.

***

Our car was an old Mercedes station wagon. The device that prevented lumps of sycamore and lurcher dogs from flying out of the back area into the passenger compartment was a retractable net. Ollie had dismantled that when *he* was a pup. But that was it, so far as Ollie's destructive instinct went. He never did demolish the kitchen (because he was fully occupied with dealing with his psychological issues). Ollie's sole in-car contribution, however, had left just three headrests as the barrier between Dylan and the rear seats, which was no barrier at all. Between the rear seats and the front seats there were two more headrests and the inviting, open alley where the gearshift sits. This was how I came to be driving along with a puppy sitting on the passenger seat intently watching the world go by via the novel perspective of the front windshield; this was how, before I knew it, I came to be driving along with a puppy sitting on my lap helping me change gears. It's not a good look. I take comfort anywhere I can, dog-owner-chic-wise. For instance, I was delighted to read that Keith Richards keeps two dogs, one old Labrador, the other a stray called Rasputin, a "little mutt" that wandered into his dressing room while the Stones were doing a gig in Moscow. Keith arranged for his people to have the animal quarantined and then shipped over to begin its new rock'n'roll lifestyle in a simple villa down in the Caribbean. "It's just like home, Rasputin, dude, but the weather's like paradise, man, and the chicks are even hotter than those pole dancers in Red Square."

This sort of hip cultural detail is the kind of thing I am always on the lookout for, and it helps, but in the real world I accept that any illusions I might have had about myself as a cool individual disappeared with the arrival of Ollie, and that the image of dog ownership is of a painfully square guy in a sweater getting worked up about a Lhasa Apso at the Westminister Dog Show, rather than Jagger and Richards getting stuck into a midnight jam. All the same, I don't actually want to be seen driving around looking as if I'm an extra from a BBC comedy-drama set in the Yorkshire Dales. So I bought a grille to reintroduce a barrier separating off the rear compartment of the car.

The grille that I had purchased fixed into the back of the wagon by the use of telescopic legs that locked by tightening the top section of the legs against the bottom, thus forcing a fit between the floor of the car and the headlining. The item is a chocolate teapot, the concept is a botch, and when you add Dylan to the equation it's a design that falls somewhat short of a minimum standard: the barrier it created was effective for up to three whole seconds.

There is no point driving around the corner from the auto-parts outlet to the Mercedes dealer for a patented factory grille—one that might actually work—because that idea is represented by the net that has already been destroyed. So I amended the grille. With the use of many bungee cords and lengths of string, rope, and twine, I tied it to the arms of the headrests. Dylan, furious at the restrictions this appeared to impose on his civil rights, set to work.

I routinely take the boys to the beach, a journey of about half an hour each way. Ollie put up with his brother in the car, provided that Dylan kept out of his personal space, which he had drawn up to represent 85 percent of the available area. This in effect annexed Dylan to the headrest end. The drive allowed Dylan a good hour in which to knuckle down to his task, more if we add in time for stopping off to pick up coffee and gas, and cans of tripe and bones. Depending on the frequency of the beach run and the associated stop-offs, the amended grille could survive for up to a week before new twine and ropes and bungee cords were required. Having studied the time and motion of this iniquitous incarceration, Dylan instigated Plan B: he set about surreptitiously dismantling the frames to which the grille was attached. Using the tried and tested stealthy teeth and saliva technique, he quietly loosened the fabric of the headrests from their internal supports. He conducted his final piece of work very quickly. One morning at a red light I turned around to see what the sinister quiet was all about. I was confronted by three metal plates sticking up out of the rear seat-backs. I had never wondered what the inside of headrests looked like, but now I knew anyway: they are holed like the drum of a washing machine, but they are flat like a certain kind of cheese grater. The car was beginning to look like it belonged to Mad Max. I gave Dylan the evil eye. Or at least I tried.

It was no use because he was thoroughly absorbed in the next stage of proceedings: he was conducting an experiment to discover whether the internal foam of a headrest can be considered edible material (it can). And Ollie? Not only does he occupy his space, he is also a good passenger. He lies comfortably on the sunny side of the car with his head slightly raised in order that he can gaze disdainfully out the window at the big dull world full of dull humans. The thought of pimping his ride is beneath his dignity; he had that one crack at it years ago, but in all honesty, he has better things to think about.

Once the headrests were gone, there were three further items that would benefit from modification: the seatbelts. And now there was a clear sight of them. Dylan could squeeze his head around the sides of the (reattached) grille. This allowed him to dispose of the outside belts. The middle seatbelt should, technically, have been beyond reach, but somehow he ate that, too. The law requires you to have functioning seatbelts throughout the cabin in order for a vehicle to be considered roadworthy. The quote for three new rear seatbelts came in at more than the old car was worth. Secondhand seatbelts were nowhere to be found. While I was considering acquiring Dylan a dog passport—so that we could drive to Germany and back and still undercut UK Mercedes main dealer prices for ancillary parts—a syndrome developed whereby the clutch pedal would suddenly sink to the floor without warning. I had to bash the gearshift into neutral to prevent stalling while trying to flirt the pedal back up to its normal position with the toe of my boot as the car kangarooed along and Dylan chirruped one of his many songs, this one an aggressive grunge rhythm in complaint at the bumpy ride. Meanwhile Ollie thumped him to tell him to shut it. None of this made for relaxing motoring. I couldn't blame Dylan for the clutch problem, at least. He had not, to the best of my knowledge, mastered that hood catch yet, and had not, therefore, contributed to the malfunction of the master cylinder. Fixing this would amount to twice the cost of a set of new seatbelts. In combination, these matters put the car beyond economic repair.

First I removed the cheese grater headrest remains, then I vacuumed it out. I emptied the vacuum *three* times, full as it was of dog hair, residual caked-on dog drool and other nonspecific dog-related fluff. After that I polished the inside with Pledge to neutralize the smell, and then I *washed* the bodywork. It looked sharp. Pausing only to introduce some air into the tires, I kangarooed it to the motor auction yard, where I explained to the staff how best to drive it on to the auction-room floor, clutchwise, to give the impression that this was one hell of a smooth ride. I walked away speculating how much it would fetch to put toward the next vehicle (which ought, really, to be an old butcher's van fitted with an internal crate). It must be worth two hundred bucks at least, maybe even three hundred. I did not bother to set a reserve price. When I returned a few days later, I was to be presented with a check for twenty dollars. *Twenty dollars.* That would not make much of a contribution toward a Ford Transit, would it? Instead, I channeled the windfall toward covering a third of the cost of a thirty-pound bag of dog food.

Happy Days

Ollie was chirpy enough when they were on the outside together taking their exercise, where, so far as his brother was concerned, he was cast into the light of the all-American hero, tough, ace at sports, and something of a ladies' man, but back home it was business as usual: Ollie was reclusive, deferential, and self-effacing. This did not suit Dylan one bit; he was far too young to be expected to relate to the concept of a Jekyll and Hyde persona in his kennel mate. Reluctant to put up with the situation, he set about changing it: he dedicated his days to "bringing Ollie out of himself." But every time he dived into his stepbrother's basket, or went in from behind with the sneaky teeth to bite him in the back of his neck, Ollie simply made himself scarce by coming up to my office in the attic where he knows I keep an emergency sofa for lying on. When Dylan followed Ollie up, I cleared him off. Now that the initial ice-breaking had taken place between them, I felt it my duty to at least partially enforce the senior animal's desires insofar as his solitude and privacy were concerned. Clearing Dylan off, though, was hopeless. He did not clear off, instead he remained outside the office door doing a Sammy Davis Jr. dance routine on the floorboards while singing "Let Me In" by the Osmonds. No man can work under these conditions. I carried him down two flights of stairs and deposited him into his main basket in the laundry room behind the kitchen, where I instructed him to "Go to sleep." I returned to work for three peaceful minutes before he struck up a tune that I could only assume was "I Shall Be Released," the live version that Dylan recorded with the Band, the most rackety rendition of this song. *Any day now, any day now . . . I shall be released . . . WhooowhoooWhooO!*

I went back downstairs and let myself out through the front door.

Yes, I could still hear him from this end of the house.

I walked around the side, adjacent to the room where Dylan was actually giving his performance. At this spot it was an impressive sonic force: the windowpanes were rattling slightly. I continued until I could no longer hear him; I was at the end of the road before this was the case. It would only be a matter of time before a representative of Norwich City Council served us with a summons re noise pollution. This was a realistic prospect—whenever Norwich City Council makes it to the national news, it is always for a skateboarding duck story. First it was because City Works had painted the shortest double yellow line in the UK; you couldn't even park a golf cart on it. "They'll be painting them up the walls next," said a local resident. The following time it was because they had banned window boxes on account of them being "dangerous," and the time after that it was because they had threatened to fell seven horse chestnut trees that lined a road near the university. The reason for this was the "risk" posed by the fallen chestnuts. And further still, children could get themselves knocked over by motorized vehicular contraptions as they made their suicidal attempts to gather the fallen chestnuts from the road.

Slapping a gag order on a singing dog seemed to me an odds-on contender for addition to this list. The more I thought about it, the more surprised I was that someone hadn't been around already.

***

I returned to our house through the back entrance. Dylan continued his warbling until I opened the door to the laundry room. I put it to him that this wasn't exactly going to sleep, was it? He treated me to the expression he was in the business of perfecting in the pursuit of his (ongoing) campaign of customizing the dining room chairs, the one that said, *It wasn't me, Officer. I wasn't even there.*

And furthermore, he seemed to say, *I'm not tired anyway.*

And moreover, he seemed to add, I WANT TO PLAY WITH OLLIE!

I gave in.

"C'mon then," I said. "It's not as if I'm getting anything done like this."

Dylan followed me up the first three stairs then shot on ahead to my closed office door, where he resumed his rendition of "Let Me In" until I arrived behind him and actually did let him in. It was time for a new approach. "Ollie," I said, "play with your brother." Dylan bounded onto the emergency sofa. Ollie looked to me for help. "No, Ollie," I said. "Sort it out yourself."

There are certain "Dylan characteristics" that allowed us all to arrive at the position whereby Ollie finally deigned to interact with another dog *indoors*, an idea that all previous history would suggest was one of the great taboos of his life.

The Dylan characteristics are as follows:

1. He is very persistent.
2. He feels no pain.
3. He is excellent at pretending to submit.
4. He does not give a monkey's arse how many times he is thrown across a room.

After Dylan had demonstrated point #1 many times over, he found that he had effectively broken Ollie's resistance and could therefore begin to enjoy the thrills of point #4. As the days passed, I began to note that Ollie looked forward to the moment when his little brother would appear for his daily drubbing. He would turn around a few times on the sofa and adopt the en garde position. He would give every sense that he was "in anticipation." He would hang off the sofa, ears pricked, listening and waiting. This was a proper turn up.

To paraphrase Harvey Keitel as the cop in pursuit of Thelma and Louise, "Writing can only get you so far, and words always run out in the end."

There's no better way of illustrating Dylan's method of persuading Ollie to discover his "inner scamp," and to get down with his bad self, than by using this picture.

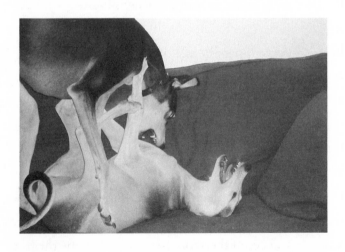

I emailed it to Karen, the breeder, under the title "Ollie and Dylan playing nicely together."

She emailed back: "He looks so happy!"

Happy Days

***

Once Ollie had decided that playing indoors was no longer on the list of restricted activity, he stopped bothering
to come to my office in order to do it. Instead he invited
Dylan into his regular domicile in Trezza's office. Here
he had territory to protect, here he could up the stakes
by defending his real bed, and here he had more space in
which to stand up in comfort (the ceiling above the sofa
in my office slopes) in the service of clamping Dylan's
head between his jaws and squeezing gently while
growling slightly. It was interesting to watch. While it
looked as though Dylan was in some sort of danger, he
really wasn't; while it was clear that Ollie could do him
any sort of damage, he really wouldn't. Here the rules
of their relationship were cemented. Even in the freaky
indoors, it was Ollie who was in charge. He would occasionally get it wrong and make Dylan cry out (not
in pain, which he does not feel, but in fright, which he
does). Ollie would pull off immediately when this signal
was given. He had no intention of hurting him. But he
had every intention of asserting his authority. If Dylan
picked up a squeaky toy, a toy that Ollie had discarded
and had taken no interest in for months, Ollie would

step forward to take it from him and drop it into his bed, where it remained, unplayed with. The same applied to any object within reach of his basket. I am a big brother myself; I recognized the form of fascism perfectly. The rationale goes as follows: I don't want it, but that does not mean that *you* can have it. Don't touch my stuff, pip-squeak.

After Dylan had exhausted every means he could find of irritating his big brother, he would fall asleep. On the rug. Beside Ollie's basket. For a time Ollie would look at Dylan intently, wearing an expression of extreme suspicion. You could see it all going through his mind: look at him, sleeping, and as if that weren't enough, beside *my* bed. What a liberty. After an hour of the intense staring he came to the conclusion that nothing was going to happen and went to sleep himself. He went to sleep with another animal slumbering in *his* own personal, and private, space. He was coming around.

The Days Get Shorter for Stan, Murphy, Tom, Tess, Holly, Bonnie, Jasper, Casper, and All the Rest . . .

Before Ollie came into my life, when the clocks were turned back all it meant to me was that the lights were switched on earlier. Now it means we have to take the second walk earlier and earlier until it practically merges with the first walk. In the shortest days of winter it's the same for everyone, and in these days, up in the meadow, when dog owners are all beating the fall of darkness together, we become part of a gang.

Stan is a chocolate Labrador, a relaxed and chill animal who is always rolling over onto his back and letting everyone have sex with him. Stan's owner is Sarah. Her catchphrase is, "Stan, you are such a tart!"

Murphy is a Staffie-cross. He was sprung from the same rescue shelter as Ollie, at about the same time. He is the kind of dog who will always be the first to go after a thrown stick (he moves like a turbo-charged hippo). With the stick clamped in his jaws, he growls at all comers to "Leave it out, or else." This is a bluff, Murphy would not harm a fly. He belongs to Brian, a character-actor type who makes side money from selling antiquarian paper on a market stall. Brian is full of jokes and always has kisses to spare for the likes of Sarah and Trezza. I am sometimes in line to receive a kiss myself, but I prefer to get my kicks by steering Brian on to the unhappy subject of the goings-on for his beloved but hapless soccer team.

Tom is the elder of the group. About ten years old, he's a handsome mutt who carries an air of gravitas about him. If he were a politician, he'd be Secretary of the Treasury. Tom belongs to Angela, who Brian thinks is "posh." Brian was astonished one day when Angela, having been bowled over from behind by the naughty black Labrador **Jasper**, was heard to exclaim, from her prone position on her backside, "Fuck it!" Jasper is all right, though Ollie and he have the occasional fight over Top Dog Dominance Issues. Tom, who knows perfectly well who is the senior animal around here, leaves them to it.

Tess also belongs to Angela. Tess turned up on the local scene one day after Angela had found her at the side of the road a few miles outside of town. Angela took her to the nearest police station, and when no one claimed her she went back to fetch her and bring her home. Tess is a pointer, an athlete who runs around in the woods doing whatever she likes and coming back in her own good time. Ollie quite fancies Tess, but she is something of a specialist at acting haughty and telling him where to stick it. You know the type.

Holly is a golden retriever. She does the littlest possible amount of exercise and considers being taken out for a walk something of an imposition on her lifestyle, which ideally involves eating chocolates while watching daytime television. Holly is owned by Fred, who is convinced that Holly fancies Dylan, though I'm not convinced that it's at all worth her while bothering herself with that kind of thought: when it comes to matters of *amore*, Dylan is a one-dog boy who sticks to Stan.

Bonnie is a liver-spot Dalmatian who is never there

at nighttime but whom we often see on the morning shift. When we first met Bonnie, her owner was on two crutches because she had injured herself "dancing at a gig." I was impressed with this as she is about my age, and if I go to a gig these days I want an assurance that the performance will take place in a seated auditorium and not end too late. Bonnie gives good sport; she will skirmish with Ollie and Dylan together at the same time. There are not all that many like her, in this specific way, though **Casper** is one. Casper is a Border terrier. Border terriers are the Energizer Bunny of dogs: they are the last ones left playing after all those running on normal batteries have long since packed it in. Casper's owner is always trying to catch the little devil; Casper puts a great deal of effort into making sure that this task is practically impossible.

The play takes place on a playing field and putting green, where there are sand traps and woods, a great adventure playground for the dogs; it's bad news for all concerned when the clocks go forward again and the ball games and putting season resume, so that where there should rightly be a dog free-for-all there are instead individuals playing miniature golf.

As the night falls to darkness the group split off their

separate ways, *a demain*. Stan, Tom, and Tess return with us up the long straight path through an avenue of trees toward where we are parked, near the prison situated at the highest point in the city—a neat Victorian cruelty, to build it where the view for the incarcerated is the very best. While Dylan and Stan continue their adolescent sexual experimentations, Tess can be glimpsed only fleetingly, in shadows. Meanwhile, Ollie and Tom set up a forward patrol, one on each flank, protecting the womenfolk and the juveniles. At their respective homes these two animals are happy to put on the disguise of the domestic pet, but in these circumstances they reveal their true natures. Here they are something quite different, here they are guards. They need no training whatsoever for this responsibility, they do it entirely as a matter of instinct.

Philip and Diddley

One Saturday we went up to the meadow where the gang of dogs usually congregates, just as the soccer scores were coming in. I sat and waited in the car until the results were read out; I cannot enter into nature until I know all the details of who has won and who has lost. Quite often I will be at a match anyway and will "allocate" this dog-walking shift to Trezza whether she likes it or not; I pay the price by doing both Sunday walks (which can be slotted in on either side of the tele-vised action).

It was a miserable afternoon, though at least I had

not traveled to the Midlands to see Stoke City play out a scintillating goalless tie at home to Luton. The weather was of the exact kind that would keep you indoors were it not that you had to go out: it was raining that persistent variety of fine English drizzle that coats the air and seems to get you wetter than a proper downpour. It would soon be dark, and Trezza and I were not surprised to find that we were the only people out. When it was just the two of them on their own, without the distraction of any other dogs, Ollie was beginning to respect Dylan as a sporting rival. Here we could see the principle, the guiding idea, as it were, beginning to come off. Ollie was happier than he used to be, he was not sulking and idle, and he was having a bad old time with his bad self and his bad brother. And Dylan loved it. He was very game, and—had Ollie only been able to see it—he was going to be a lot faster than him, and soon, too. Dylan was six months old now and already had the zero-to-sixty miles per hour of a Jaguar. The rhythm his pads made on turf was like the percussion of 2,000 wild turkeys thundering by. It was only Ollie's experience, combined with Dylan's deference, that was enabling Ollie to stay on top of the situation. Breeding aside, Dylan had enjoyed a start in life that was the opposite of Ollie's. Dylan was loved, sheltered, nurtured, and fed like a prince. Ollie, by contrast, had been found by a dog warden in Thetford Forest when he was a couple of months old. He must have been a mess, because the staff at the Dogs Trust rescue shelter thought he might have rickets when they first saw him. I believe there was some doubt over whether he'd pull through.

It is the golf course that comprises the biggest and best (for dog walkers) part of the meadow. None of the usual gang was in evidence and so Ollie and Dylan continued to make their own fun. In the descending gloom they began using a sand trap in the same way that skateboarders use a half-pipe. It elevated my spirits to watch them. Dylan suddenly stopped dead in mid-vert and landed on all fours, where he remained in the stopped-dead position for a microsecond before belting off into the trees. "Dylan," we called after him, to no avail. I hadn't yet got around to whistle-training him. He was given to a certain increasingly large amount of disobedience, which was not a great combination in conjunction with his speed. He was becoming noticeably faster by the day; if you tried to photograph him on the move, this was your great picture:

A portrait of the artist as a young dog.

The top of his head was already on its way, exit frame north, and the rest of his body was stretched out right behind him. He could even kick off in a different direction in mid-flight, as though air was solid, as though his pads could gain traction on it. The catalyst for his acrobatics on this occasion was Diddley, the young Dalmatian. This was their first meeting. Ollie looked sharply at the scene for a moment before hosing up behind Dylan, as if to menace Diddley. In a developing trait, he was behaving as older siblings often do: *he* was allowed to batter his brother, but this was his exclusive right. Should any other dog try it on, there would be himself to deal with. Ollie is an absolute featherweight, sleek and feminine-looking, but that is all so much deception and disguise. He has lived on his wits, he is streetwise, he is the Sugar Ray Leonard of his manor. Philip emerged out of the gloom behind his charge. I began to make noises explaining Ollie's behavior: he's only looking out for the youngster, he's fine, really, he's not actually aggressive (although it may seem otherwise).

"That's all right, boy," Philip said. "They'll sort themselves out."

To me, that is the perfect response in a first-time meeting with a new dog owner. It is the opposite of the type you note walking freely along in the mid-distance and whom you note putting their dog on to a leash as they in turn note you. They do not do this because their animal is timid or aggressive, they do it because they don't want it playing. Sometimes they even mention the fact. "He only wants to play," they say, as the dog pulls toward you, wagging its tail at the end of the leash. They shake their heads at the incomprehensibility of their animal's bizarre impulse as they drag the poor mutt away behind them. Still, at least they don't pick it up, like some do.

Diddley and Dylan were soon engaged in a rumble, a hybrid activity somewhere between wrestling and steeplechasing.

"D'you mind if I come along with you?" Philip said. "I could do with tiring him out."

"No problem," I said. In a gesture of dog-owner-to-dog-owner kinship, Philip offered me a cigarette, a roll-up out of a tin. I put my hand up in friendly no thanks. "Not before the first drink," I said.

Philip looked at me curiously. Tobacco and alcohol fumes were billowing off him. It's one of my favorite combination smells, one that takes me straight back to my early life, to my uncles, from when I was a kid. It is the smell of my father's brothers (there were three), along with my grandfather, tumbling into my grandmother's kitchen after the Sunday lunchtime session. "It's burnt offerings," Grandmother would say, as she pulled their meals from the oven. They were not burnt offerings actually; she went out of her way to keep the beef moist by turning one plate over to cover another and flooding it with gravy. The scent of booze and cigs is not only more recognizable and more heady in the afternoon than it is later on, it's actually *different* in the light of day than it is after nightfall. I noted a convincing horizontal scar under Philip's right eye. I noted his slightly louche, rolling gait. I could translate his curious look in one way: it's never too early for the first drink,

boy, ergo how can it ever be too early for the first cigarette? And this would be the correct translation. Some
months later I drove Philip down to Cheltenham, to the
horse races. We set off early, just after 7 a.m. Philip
told me that he'd already had a couple of beers before
I picked him up.

"Really?" I said.

"Best time of day for it, boy," he replied. "When the
blackbirds are singing."

There was a pause in the wrestling while Ollie conducted a thorough investigation of Diddley's rear end
and reproductive parts. This seemed to settle everything
once and for all. Diddley was simply a kid, and so Dylan
and Diddley were allowed to be friends, a matter that
Ollie could sanction while preferring, for the most part,
to remain aloof from their immature childishness. While
the youngsters messed around chewing each other's ears
and testing who could jump the highest, who could get
the muddiest, who could fling whom the farthest, and
who could go fastest (with Dylan occasionally trying his
luck at mounting Diddley), Ollie indulged the sensitive
side of his nature by investigating the wide range of exotic smells that collect around the foot of trees. All the
while he kept a weather-eye open lest any other animal

should come within range of the, not one, but two, adolescents that were now under his jurisdiction.

Philip was taken with our dogs. He had not quite seen their like before, but then nobody has ever seen one like Ollie. His coat gleams over his supermodel frame. He looks, as Philip later put it, "like a giant mole, boy."

"What you been doing this afternoon, then?" Philip asked. I had been working on a book, but I did not say that. I had also had half an ear out to the soccer commentaries, and had taken a break a couple of times to watch horse races on television. I said this.

"Ah!" he said. "Are you into the horses, boy? I been down the bookies this morning and watching television most of the afternoon with a few beers: done all right."

Directly after imparting this information he went on to talk about this "system" that he'd once had, which he was thinking about resurrecting. To me, that was not a good sign. Having a system is tantamount to announcing that you are a maniac. There *is* no system, and if studying the formbook worked, then we could all give up our day jobs and be as rich as Croesus.

"I'll tell you what," I said, "I'm not the greatest gambler going . . ."

"Neither am I, boy," he said. "Not many of us are, boy."

". . . because I'm one of those soppy individuals who forms attachments to horses and who will back them because I like them and against the mass of available counter-information offered as a warning against such a course of action as evidenced by all previous history and experience."

Trezza mentioned a chaser named Ollie Magern, an animal that stood as a shorthand for everything I'd just said, and that also gave a clue as to another method of gambling I occasionally use: by name. "Only grannies use that 'system,' boy," Philip said months later when I advised him of a (placed) horse that I'd backed (at long odds) called Jack the Blaster, after my son, under this scheme. And now, at this first meeting, he laughed in the face of my amateur admission vis-à-vis backing on the "affection method." *But*, he said—mature, hardened, and professional gambler that he was—he *too* held the animals in high regard and fondness, respected the effort they put in on our behalf, and that, even against his better instincts, and his *system*, and although he wouldn't admit it, he couldn't say that he'd never thought of gambling like that, once or twice, not if all truth be told, boy.

"Do you come here often?" he asked as we made our way back to where the car was parked.

"Pretty often," I said.

"I'll see you then," he said. "I'm always around."

***

That was not entirely true, because if he was always about I would have met him before.

"What did you make of him?" I asked Trezza as we ushered Ollie and Dylan into the car.

"Just what you need, a gambling adviser. I liked him," she said.

As we drove away, the atmosphere in the back of the car was strangely quiet. Dylan tends to remain alert and upstanding, post-walk, in case there are any dogs being taken around the block on leashes, unfortunate creatures who need barking at in sympathy for their wretched plight: what kind of so-called exercise is *that*? But now he was spent. Playing with Diddley had exhausted him: this was both happy news and a happy sight. Things were strangely quiet, but in a good way. We would catch up with Diddley again. Dylan and Diddley would each be exactly the mate that the other was looking for to make life complete.

Squirrels, Foxes, Nature, and Other Hazards

From the youngest age, Dylan was introduced to our old friends Milla and Leo—a Doberman and an elderly Labrador retriever, respectively. Leo, like his owner, John, is an English gent, charming and polite to just the right degree: Leo ignores and discards Dylan's act, as he does with most juveniles. When he sees our group approach he potters over to me for the handout from my pocket, and that's that.

Milla, on the other hand, is Ollie's age. From Dylan's point of view Milla is his big brother's excellent friend, the one who will actually condescend to play with him.

It is Milla who Dylan selects to test whether it is possible to hitch a ride on the tail of another dog. Milla—a rescue from the streets of London—has a docked tail: it is Milla's slightly superior speed and the tantalizing proximity of the tail stump that provokes Dylan into stretching to hold on to it with his teeth, into using it as a tow-hook. Milla is not as menacing as he looks; he will let Dylan get away with this liberty-taking for much longer than I would, if I were him. In so doing, Milla demonstrates the ways of the pack: he recognizes Dylan's age, and his relationship to his good friend Ollie, and so he dutifully acts out the role of indulgent elder. But even without the Ollie factor, it might be much the same. The senior dogs do not turn on the juniors until it is absolutely necessary, until they become unruly teenagers who need to be put in their places with a severe telling off. Perhaps we could reintroduce these codes to human society, I sometimes think, especially after I have been listening to the talk of dog walkers for too long. A good percentage of these are Grumpy Old Men, and they hold the views of that generation: a smack on the side of the head never did them any harm, and all the rest of it.

"These fields we are walking in are 80 percent more dangerous than they used to be," Jeff, Milla's owner, advises me. He proceeds to spout the far right's talking points verbatim, as if an elite squad of hip-hop-loving criminal masterminds were surrounding us even as we speak, holed up in the brambles, waiting to relieve us of our collars and leashes. "You would get on well with my dad," I say to Jeff, as a way of avoiding direct engagement with any of his Atilla-like views. John simply blows his nose. They all want locking up, all except Milla, of course. This is what Jeff means. Milla routinely mugs my pockets without suffering any kind of sanction.

But these "political debates" seldom run to a conclusion because every avenue opens up a by-road.

"Where did this happen then, Jeff?" I ask, when he tells me about a council that has subsidized the building of a mosque by using money that it raised by closing down a nursery school. "Wolverhampton, was it? Sorry to see *they* lost again last night (not)." All topics can be diverted into much more important discussions concerning soccer. These are conversations that seldom get finished either because, hold on a second: where the hell is Dylan?

He may only be young, he may only be a junior, but that does not mean that he is not a fierce, brave hunter.

Fetching Dylan

There are woods all around the sports fields at the back of the university, where these meet-ups take place. Dylan makes it his business to see that no squirrels are allowed to go about their normal routines in those woods, not without receiving a fright followed by a howled warning regarding their general conduct. He is a busybody, a self-appointed patroller of forests, and even with an unbroken voice he could produce a convincing simulation of a wolf. I was seated at a dinner function once where I was happy to discover that my neighboring diner and I shared a mutual hero in Bob Dylan. I was saying how I'd been to see him at a gig at a stadium in the north a few years earlier, and that at some point during the concert I'd had the passing thought that if a Martian had landed in our midst he would have scratched his Martian head and wondered how it could possibly be that one of the crowd of Earthlings couldn't make a better noise than the one on stage. My fellow diner contributed his own anecdote by telling me how he'd recently caught one of Dylan's shows at the Brixton Academy. He said that as he left the venue he turned to his friends to comment on the ordeal by saying, "Well, that was absolutely awful, wasn't it?" In the developing theme, one of the friends was able to trump *him*: "If you think *that* was bad, you

74

should have heard him last year at Hammersmith." All of those involved in these anecdotes are Dylan *fans*. And they all stayed to the end of the shows, too—I noted that. John and Jeff are fans of Dylan the dog, and they, too, stay until he is safely returned to the pack. Still: by crikey, they both say, in their own ways, looking toward the woods, "He can't half make a bloody racket though."

He continued to shoot from tree to tree. In glimpses (and howling aside), it was worth noting his approach to his duties: he conducted the activity on his hind legs, bouncing through the undergrowth with his tail flashing vertically like the conductor rod at the back of a bumper car.

I called his name, to no avail.

"Ollie," I said, in an excited put-on voice, "where's Dylan?"

My hope was that this would encourage Ollie to go and retrieve him for me. Ollie would look in the general direction of Dylan and then look at me. It's not my problem, he seemed to say. I fail to understand why you felt the need to introduce him into the family in the first place.

Though Ollie is an expert at this pretense of grandeur, he is no angel himself, as he has demonstrated by setting a bad example to Dylan in several ways.

For instance, the following routine:

1. Smell fox poop in the distance.
2. Tear off to the source and roll on your back with your legs flailing in the air to get yourself fully coated. All the while turning a deaf ear to your master.
3. As your master nears, yelling his peculiar foreign words and shaking his fist, run behind a hedge.
4. If you see Jeff and John approaching in the distance, belt up to them in a friendlier-than-usual manner. See if you can't get them to stroke you before your master gets his warning in, too late.

This activity is supposed to be in the interests of scent-masking: they do it so that they can hunt the fox without the fox catching on that *they* are dogs. All well and good, except that on the single occasion I have seen Ollie come face-to-face with a fox (cub), all that happened was that the two of them conducted a seven-minute staring competition before going their separate ways.

Dylan is a very quick learner. It took him no time at all to get the hang of "rolling." After one particularly thorough effort, he approached Jeff and John looking for the stroke. They did not need a warning from me this time. He had found a very fresh batch from a very prolific fox. Apart from the warning-cloud flies that were encircling him, he looked, as Jeff put it, "as though he'd been caught up in an oil slick."

"You're a *good boy*, aren't you, Dylan," says Jeff.

"Yes, well done, boy," says John. "That'll teach those foxes to leave their mess lying around."

Back in the car I keep a box of wet wipes in order to deal with the aftermath of such rolling incidents. If I use about fifteen of these and then open all the windows and the sunroof, and switch the fan on high, I am able to drive home without being asphyxiated. The dogs don't seem to understand that it is the rolling that earns them "the bucket," for if they did they would surely cut it out. The scent of fox lingers in their coat and pelt for days, though it can be vaguely neutralized by rubbing tomato ketchup in with the shampoo, before finishing "the bucket" off with something that is even worse: the hose. They stand dripping and trembling and thinking vile thoughts: *they are cruel and heartless these humans, make no mistake. They'll be giving us a bowl of food apiece and a couple of pig's ears next, the bastards.*

***

All of the aforementioned is fairly harmless: squirrels, with their cheating, vertical ways, can never be caught; the smell of fox poop evaporates from a pelt in time.

But there is a real and great danger on the university campus. It appears in spring, is much more prevalent in the evening than it is in the morning, and comes in the form of rabbits. Ollie's efforts, in this respect, are half-baked. Though he was never much good at the sport, in terms of actual picking up, he used to be keen on the chase; now he barely looks their way.

But they drive Dylan insane. As the days warm up and the population multiplies, they litter the grounds of the campus like figures in a modern-art installation. This turns the matter of letting Dylan off the leash into a huge gamble. While out with Trezza one evening, he picked up a supine baby rabbit. Trezza instructed him to drop it. He jumped back from her, the rabbit feet dangling out either side of his mouth like a cuddly toy. This did not make a good impression in a public space, and students, particularly female foreign students, would sometimes scream when confronted with such a spectacle. But Dylan would not give the kill up. Instead he continued to jump backward while he crunched it between his jaws, never once dropping it, until it had disappeared practically whole down his throat. The following day his first dump was normal, his second, which was not far behind the first, came out Velcro-wrapped in a fur coat. That was all the harm that had been caused (to him): his constitution is cast-iron. If Ollie ate like that you could expect several visits to the vet and diarrhea for three weeks.

It is not the consuming of rabbit that constitutes the danger; it is the chasing. The campus has internal roads: the potential for death is obvious as Dylan dives headlong after the rabbits, one after another after another, hell-bent on going wherever it is that they go. Mainly this is into the safety of their warrens, but there are those idiot rabbits who end up being momentarily caught like a rabbit in headlights as the oncoming bus looms down. Actually, they don't linger long in the face of this imminent death because they are more frightened of Dylan than the bus. In this way the rabbits lead him out of the danger that they have got him into in the first place, but the whole business does nothing for my heart, nor for anyone's image: allowing an animal loose to behave like that is about as good a look as having a pup sitting on your lap helping you steer a beat-up Mercedes.

The campus is a village made of many buildings. The rabbits take him around the back of these, where they can escape down their slip roads into their warrens. Dylan disappears behind the vast rectangular hangar that is the Sainsbury Centre for Visual Arts. And then he is nowhere to be seen. Five minutes elapse; ten minutes elapse. I begin to feel panic. Suddenly there is a sighting, a flash of him between the triangular accommodation blocks of the ziggurats. I call him, but he hears nothing. For practical purposes he is deaf now; it has gone well beyond a battle of the wills between animal and master. At home, indoors, he can put on a thoroughly convincing charade of being a domestic animal, but here, now, he is answering the other, much more urgent, side of his nature. He is bred from a coursing line; he is putting into practice that which he cannot help. Eventually— and nothing to do with me—after fifteen minutes, he stops. He looks my way, as though seeing me for the first time in his life. Where am I? he appears to say. Who am I? he appears to say. He is coming down from the high;

rabbits are to Dylan what cocaine used to be for Wall Street bankers—an unstoppable, addictive compulsion.

He comes to my hand for a treat. I take his collar. He seems happy to be put on the leash, to be exonerated from having to do any more of that exhausting hunting. He has become pet-like again, and, fortunately for all concerned, he is still alive.

One definition of insanity is repeating the same action over and over again and expecting a different result. I proceeded a short way down this road, thinking I could "train" Dylan out of his instinct, before I had to demonstrate to myself that I was not beyond hope. I made the demonstration by banning all visits to the university campus in the evenings.

Sand Hounds

As an alternative to the perilous life around the groves of academe, we headed east. Half an hour's drive away on the Norfolk coast—the time that Dylan spent so diligently working toward his BA in Vehicle Scrapping—lies the remote village of Winterton-on-Sea. Here is a beautiful beach, a wide, spare expanse where the sand is fine underfoot. If you think back to their origins with the Bedouin tribesmen, it's obvious that Salukis are desert dogs. Sand says something fundamental to them: like fish introduced to water, they are in their element. They are in their element, though each in his different way. As an illustration of their opposed natures, where the surface underfoot has Ollie prancing like Nijinsky, Dylan thunders back and forth like Red Rum on a free gallop. His movements are so wild, featuring so many chicanes and double-backs, that he is frequently to be seen running at full speed on three legs with the fourth hind leg being pressed into action to simultaneously scratch at his head—he is an expert at flicking sand into his own eyes and has developed a technique that means he can remove it while he remains on the run.

Both of them refuse to go into the sea: water is wet and dangerous—it is not for them; it is for dolphins. It does, though, supply one source of sport; onshore winds blow foam from the breakers in large cluster bubbles: these are excellent for chasing across the sand, if you are Dylan. Then there is driftwood, old rope, abandoned lobster pots, lengths of beached timber, and all the rest of it to discover and investigate. After that there are any number of surprise snacks that come in the form of half-dead crabs, deceased fish, and guano (neither of the latter is out of the question in rolling terms, either, not by any means). And usually there are other canines to meet and greet, in a holiday spirit. Some of these, so far as Dylan is concerned, may be up to half a mile away, just specks in the distance. His usual technique is to go three-quarters of the way there before coming over, slightly wary and belting all the way back to where Ollie is waiting to batter him for his disobedience: Ollie notes that Dylan refuses to heed my calls—while that may be acceptable behavior in his case, it is a different matter for the kid. In these ways, by the time I have walked a mile, to the highest dune where a hippie Maypole has been erected—our agreed turning point—Dylan has put in a seven-mile shift. The Maypole is a continually evolving sculpture to which many plastic containers and other assorted items of sea debris are attached by old rope and multicolored twine. It is not pretty, but it is there.

***

Behind the beach, the wide-ranging dunes create a landscape that stands in absolute contrast to the flat sweep of sand that runs away to the tide. We were out there one cold February evening, in the hour before dark. From the top of the highest dune you can see for miles. To the east the sky was banded in three shades of midnight blue, to the west in four shades of crimson. Naked winter trees stood stark against one horizon, the sails of a windfarm were stopped to attention against another. A heavy mist sat on the lowest ground like steam; the higher slopes and the tops of the dunes were all that were visible. We were the only living souls there (apart from the rabbits and birds and foxes). Ollie and Dylan dived into the silver mist to reappear a hundred yards away where they stood silhouetted on the top of a dune like a couple of stags. Their breath pumped into the air, heat rose from their coats. I felt lucky to see this world of theirs, as well as the many other worlds that I've encountered while we have been out walking, worlds created by weather and nature. We got caught in such a storm out at the farthest point of our walk one summer night that I had to drive home wearing only my underpants and a spare bomber jacket that I had accidentally, and fortunately, left in the car. My pants were so wet that when I pulled them off and held them in front of me the legs continued to leak like downspouts, and when I tipped my boots up, water poured from them. We'd jogged back to the car in a group, Ollie and Dylan staying close beside me, repeatedly attempting to shake the rain off themselves and repeatedly looking at me as if it were my fault. Couldn't I make it stop? What was the point of me? At the parking lot they leaped into the car, where they sat slick like a pair of seals. Dylan blinked water out of eyes, which were wild in astonishment at my stupidity for taking him out at this ridiculous moment, and at the weather itself. We had all run harder as the finish line came into sight, and it was Dylan who had put the most effort into trying to dodge the individual drops of the downpour. Ollie glowered at me. How many times do we have to go through this, Master; how many times do you need to be told: you shouldn't take a dog out on a day like this.

During Dylan's first full winter I watched a whole storm barrier disappear on Winterton beach. It became buried over the course of just two months as each day

Two months later this barrier was buried.

the tide deposited sand in vast amounts. Coastal erosion is all we ever hear about, but there is coastal deposition, too. Without the dogs I would have no knowledge of this; without the dogs I would never see any of it.

That winter, our beach walk developed into a daily routine. I became addicted to it, most particularly in the hour before nightfall, an hour that takes place between half past three and half past four during the shortest days. Writing is not a nine-to-five life: this is the happy fact that allowed me to take to the road at three o'clock in order to satisfy the addiction. My earliest editor and tutor, the poet George Szirtes, once mentioned something that had been said about the American laureate Robert Frost, which was this: "Scratch the surface, and underneath you'll find an Arctic waste."

"I like that," I said. "What's it supposed to mean?"

"It means that at some level writers are bastards," George replied. "Someone dies, they think: hmm, what can I make of that?"

There is a definite and rather unappealing truth in this. Still, you pay the price for your bastardly, Arctic Robert Frost–like tendencies because, on the other hand (from apparently having endless free time), the job is always there, stalking your every waking hour, waiting to be done. The work never stops, which is both a blessing—any activity may be defined as "research"—and a curse: you never really switch off. On those rare occasions when you do manage it—halfway through a concert, let's say—you can be sure that your subconscious will switch you back on again at the earliest possible opportunity (look at that woman, look at the way she's sitting in that painful, odd posture: that is *exactly* how the character in the short story you've been thinking of writing must sit!). But for me, at least, it's fair to say that the great compensation for waking every morning to the immediate thought that you need to write enough before nightfall to qualify for the description "a day's work" (and the knowledge that *not* doing so will make you miserable all the way to bedtime) is that I can slack off at any time. I feel fortunate to be able to call this arrangement my "timetable."

***

During the drive out east, and in between his bouts of destruction, Dylan would chirrup and sing and wail his songs, songs that I imagined were all called, one way or another, "Are We There Yet?!" It was very annoying. Though I have never wanted to live outside the safe hubbub of a city—if I'm there for any length of time, I begin to find the sparseness of the population and the quietness of the countryside disturbing and unnatural— I started sniffing about at properties near those dunes simply as a possible way of eliminating Dylan's racket. It was a din there seemed to be no way of stopping: telling him to zip it just made him think you were joining in, which had the undesirable side effect of encouraging him to become more enthusiastic in his vocal delivery. We bought a can of "dog control" from a pet shop, a pressurized spray can with a nozzle that blasted out a jet of compressed air. Dogs are supposed to dislike this and indeed Dylan wasn't keen. It quieted him right down. Once. The next time he simply ducked behind the backseats and carried on singing from there, in a rather unnatural position that enabled him to access a whole new range of basso profundo.

Things were different on the way back, though. Here, silence reigned, because:

Dylan can fly from the top of one dune to the top of the next without touching down. This irritates Ollie, it forces him to think and to be strategic—activities that he does not care for. He has to work hard to kill off all the angles in order that he can check the young pretender and keep him in his place. The fact of the matter is that, ever since he passed the six-month mark, Dylan has been more than capable of outpacing the older dog, who is no slouch himself. But Ollie broke a leg when he was three, and lost half a yard as a consequence of that injury. Still, Ollie sticks to his task. Once he has cut the corner enough times to deplete Dylan's reserves of energy, he exploits the situation by chasing him down and burning him out. He is not happy until Dylan sinks to the ground panting in submission. The expression "blow his lungs up" flashed through my mind more than once in the months leading up to Dylan's first birthday, but the danger of that had gone, I think, once he had turned eight or nine months: he is one of those animals who appears to have an indestructible constitution. And anyway, he prepares for his exercise with a proper warm-up, doesn't he—he keeps his breathing apparatus in the pink by tuning it up with all those damn singing exercises en route.

Once Ollie is satisfied that he has put Dylan in his place he wanders off lonely as a cloud to be supercilious and aloof. There are, of course, many rabbits in those dunes, and it is to these that Dylan switches his attention just as soon as he has his third wind. The further great attraction of this arena for me is that there are no roads or buildings to go with the rabbits; the place is safe. Well, safe apart from this: some owners won't take their dogs out there because of the snakes that sometimes emerge to give a dog a nasty bite. But, as I have never seen a snake myself, I refuse to believe in them, a position I have been forced to adopt because we need *somewhere* for a workout and I am running out of options.

No-Go Zones

The following areas have all had to be put on the restricted access list:

1. The local woods
Reason: too small. The distance from the center to the surrounding roads is no more than one hundred and fifty yards or, to put it another way, seven seconds. Dylan has been out on the road more than once. I have not exactly notified Trezza of this (to avoid accusations centered around "lack of responsibility" issues), but I have mentioned the general idea of "road danger" and she has

agreed to rule the woods out, too. This matter has been in her mind, anyway. She becomes very overanxious if Dylan strays out of sight; she even frets when he is in the trees giving the squirrel population the benefit of his opinions (okay, so you can't see him, but anyone within a three-mile radius will be aware that he is alive and kicking). The particular road that Dylan has explored (twice) is situated in a suburban setting at the bottom end of the woods where it is all detached thirties housing with little, leaded windowpanes, and semis with tidy front yards. This road is a cul-de-sac and sees almost no traffic, though *almost* is the key word here. The top end of the woods opens on to a slightly different world. Here there is public housing, near to where Philip was brought up. Philip says it can be quite rough up there, but to me it looks relatively tame. It is one of my instinctive reactions when people tell me that areas are rough, or dodgy, to play the "I'm from Stoke-on-Trent" card. This is a form of self-defense, one that means "I've seen it all, I am impossible to impress, and I don't scare easily either." I omit to play the "I'm from Stoke-on-Trent, I've seen it all, and I'm a very good runner, what with all the practice I've had at running away from the stuff I've seen" card. Philip grew up one block farther along from the buildings at the top of these woods. He advised me that he was the hardest fighter on that block, and that as a matter of fact he was the hardest fighter in all Norwich, too, ask anyone. A certain number of the dogs from up on the top end of the woods share Philip's talent, which is another reason to skip the area. Not that Ollie isn't an excellent scrapper himself, as we shall see later, sadly. It's not Ollie I'm thinking about, in terms of aggression, it's Dylan. For all his mouthiness and athleticism, when it all kicks off, Dylan shoots into the place of safety between my legs. He is a lover, not a fighter.

2. The meadow with the nearby putting green

Like the woods, the meadow is also bordered by roads on all sides. Though these are technically, and realistically, far enough out of reach not to cause undue anxiety, Dylan did once escape onto the property at the far side of the place. He had chased a female (rescue) greyhound. The greyhound's owner was one of these taciturn individuals that you regularly encounter in the dog world; you give them an instant character profile: serial killer. He refused eye contact and said very little as I stood calling Dylan, whistling and clapping, expecting him to return with his new friend at any moment even as

I looked in vain in the direction of the trees into which they'd disappeared. The taciturn owner finally advised me of "what would have happened," because, he said, she was "always doing that" and he'd "just about had enough of her."

"What would have happened?" I asked. "What is she always doing?"

She was always legging it all the way back home was what, because she tended to "take fright of other dogs."

"Where do you live?" I asked.

He informed me of the rough address and then began trudging back in the direction of it while cursing to himself. I held a strong view regarding the amount of time he'd allowed to elapse before he released the crucial information about "what would have happened," but I kept that to myself as I ran down a path and toward some steps that lead out onto a parade of shops, and hence to the tidy group of houses that had been named. Ollie had picked up on the details of the situation and trotted alongside me looking suitably appalled and also looking a picture of obedience. He was at least as bad as Dylan at this kind of activity when he was a youngster— he was the career criminal of the game, a habitual offender and a recidivist—but you would never know it now. At the top of the steps I caught sight of Dylan. He was beside a van, being held by the collar by a man who was phoning the number on his tag.

"You want to be careful, mate," the man said. "I nearly knocked him down."

Something in the van caught my attention, which was two terriers sitting in the cab, one climbing on the other's back, the better to observe the goings-on of these weird immigrant types. We had been lucky. Dylan had been nearly run over by a dog lover, one who had acted in all the right ways.

"He's never done that before (not here, anyway). He's only a youngster," I said, by way of half-baked exoneration. "He was chasing this greyhound," I continued, by way of explanation.

"A black one, a bitch?" the man asked.

"Yes," I said.

"She's always doing that, she is," he said.

"So I hear," I said. I thanked him, returned Dylan and Ollie to their leashes, and headed back to the meadow and over to the other side where the car was parked. I was a bit shaken by this episode; I decreed our walk "over." Safe places for us to go were becoming fewer by the day. I looked down at Dylan. I was pretty furious with him, but at the same time I was delighted he was still alive; the last thing I wanted was to see him flattened by a truck. I would need to buy a bloody farmhouse with acres of land around it to afford myself peace of mind, the way he was performing. He would end up costing me a hundred grand in mortgage penalties and would force me to live in the countryside, too, a concept that I was even more against now that I had looked at a couple of barn conversions out near Winterton. These residences were "luxury" all right, but the more I stood there considering living in a flat landscape beside salt marshes in the middle of nowhere, the more I was against it. I'd go mad. We'd be safest living in the desert with Bedouins, where there are no bloody roads at least. While I was having these stray thoughts I noted that Ollie was looking daggers at his stepbrother. You stupid boy, he seemed to be saying. He savaged Dylan around the back of his neck. Try not to cost us our liberty in the future or I'll have to kill you, he seemed to be saying.

3. The university campus

Already on the list because of the rabbits. But only in the evenings and at night. We could still go there in the

morning while the rabbits were sleeping in and there
was plenty of distraction on offer in the way of Milla.

***

With any open ground that was in striking distance of
our immediate locale ruled out of bounds, it was small
wonder that I was practically a beach bum by now.

Philip, Denman, and the Cops

Denman is a racehorse. He is part owned by the flamboyant professional gambler Harry Findlay, who has nicknamed him "The Tank." It is clear from the nickname what kind of animal he is. The Tank is trained by champion trainer Paul Nicholls. Nicholls has the 2007 Gold Cup winner, Kauto Star, in his stable as well as Denman. They live in adjacent boxes and are considered the best pair of chasers in training by some large distance. Denman, though the same age, is a year behind Kauto Star in career terms. Kauto is the reigning champ by virtue of his Gold Cup title, a race in which he cruised to victory in 2007, a year he completely dominated by winning everything in sight. The two will run against each other in the Gold Cup on its next renewal. The Tank is Joe Frazer to the Star's Muhammad Ali; the former is a bruiser, the latter an artist. They are both fantastic animals, and Nicholls—who has done the business of "anticipation" a huge favor—has stated an aim, which he achieves, of keeping them apart until a meeting becomes inevitable. That day will arrive at Cheltenham on March 14, 2008. Though there will be fifteen horses involved, the public will see the contest as a simple confrontation between the title-holder and the pretender. It is the most keenly awaited head-to-head in racing for years; in the months leading up to the showdown, acres of newsprint will be dedicated to punditry and speculation. Kauto is the even-money favorite; Denman is no more than two-to-one; the next horse, Exotic Dancer, is fourteen-to-one. The rest you can have at any price.

***

One thing that singles you out as a professional, committed gambler is that you "take a view." Philip has taken the view that Denman will beat Kauto Star in the

Big One. Once the view has been taken, the matter must be offered into the public domain and put up for discussion and debate with due frequency. Over an eight-month period—the time between Philip's first mention of his "view" and the actual running of the race—I will spend many hours considering the merits of Denman re Kauto, and eventually I will take a view of my own.

For now it is only my second encounter with Philip and Diddley. It is here, and over our subsequent early meetings, that I will discover a certain large amount of information. A particular matter has crossed my mind since we first met in the meadow, which is this: Philip has said that he is "always around, boy," yet I have never seen him before, and I am around often enough myself. This is a mystery that Philip soon solves. He is only recently always around because he is excluded from the area on the other side of Norwich where he normally lives. He must not go within several hundred meters of his home address by order, because he has caused a bit of a stir by taking the law into his own hands and beating up some drug dealers in the apartments along the way from his own place. Philip may drink, a lot, but he is against drug dealers because "they are scum" and they "bring a lot of other scum into the area."

"Are you in trouble, then?" I ask him. "Do you have to go to court?"

"Oh yes, boy," he says. "Certainly."

***

The matter of Philip's court case becomes common knowledge among the dog-walking population. Now that he has arrived, Philip certainly *is* always around. He walks Diddley for hours on end, and in no time at all he and his companion become the subject du jour among the regulars in the meadow. Soon enough everyone is asking whether you have met this Philip character, with his Dalmatian, and soon enough everyone's answer to the inquiry is yes.

I have a follow-up question about the court appearance, one that runs along the lines of "Have you ever been up before the judge before?"

I believe he will answer in the affirmative. It's a tip, as Philip would have it: the sure bet of the day.

As indeed it is.

Over the months ahead, Philip, who as well as being loquacious can also be quite physically expressive, amuses me many times in the process of bringing me up to date with his autobiographical details. His stories often start in the middle, an approach to narrative that I'm fond of, and are often fractured in terms of their time sequence, another technique I admire, though this does provoke many moments when things become difficult to follow. On one particular occasion, while we are standing on the field next to the prison (which is adjacent to the meadow, and provides a daily reminder of where he might end up), he is telling me about the time when the police descended on his home address from all directions. "They was running around like the bleedin' Keystone Cops, boy. And it wan't hardly anything what I did, either: I couldn't believe it."

As Philip found himself surrounded, the principle negotiating officer was heard to announce his hope that "there wouldn't be a repeat of all that trouble like they had last time."

"No, no trouble," Philip said. He turned to me and made a gesture, stretching his arms down behind his back, touching his wrists together at his waist, palms facing outward. "Cuff me up," he said he'd advised the negotiating officer. "I'm going quiet," he said.

I could picture the incident, which was well told, and nicely mimed, but there was a bigger question that remained in the air, one that I picked up.

"What 'trouble last time' Philip?"

Philip often tells the same story several times over. I like repetition, too: I am interested in the way that, with many people, not just with Philip, the details will change slightly with each telling. Memory is unreliable. I mention this to him. "Oh, that," he says. "That's what led to so many arguments. About who owes who money."

The best version of this "trouble last time" episode came when we took the dogs on a trip, a couple of months after he'd described it in the first instance.

Philip can sometimes be a little slurry and slightly off his feet. He can even sometimes be outright drunk, for which he will apologize. He is an expert on lager: he can describe the subtle differences in flavors and effects between brands, depending whether they are brewed under license or in the country of origin, in the same way others talk about wine. He avoids what he calls "the top shelf," though. "Whenever I buy a bottle of vodka, that ends up costing me a thousand bucks," he says, "what with all the fines and summonses that come along with it." The earlier in the day, the less likelihood there is of any of this.

One morning, when I was still getting to know him, I found him perfectly sober and in an unusually introverted mood. We'd crossed paths maybe five or six times by now. As we were nearing the end of the walk he let on that he had a collector coming around for sixty bucks that day, and that he didn't have a button to pay him off. "It's crazing me, boy," he said. "I've been out here since five o'clock this morning thinking how to sort it. But there's just no way." He didn't actually ask, of course, but he was very subtly leaning on me. We walked on a bit. "Listen," I said, "meet me up at the ATM in fifteen minutes."

It was pouring by the time we were outside the branch of Lloyds, where a dripping wet Diddley was overexcited to be catching sight of us again so soon; Ollie and Dylan stared out the car window intently. Poor Diddley. At least they were in the warm and dry, unlike some of their kind. I took a hundred out, forty for me, sixty for Philip. I didn't have his cell phone number, and this was not the moment to ask for it: that would signal a lack of trust, though in truth, part of me thought this would be the last I'd ever see of either him or the cash. Once in a while I have money to chuck about, mostly not. I didn't tell Trezza, so I guess this happened during normal times. "Thanks, boy," Philip said. "That's what I'd have done," he said, meaning the extra score, and I believed him on that.

I did see him again, the following day, of course, what with him always being around, and soon enough I picked up his cell phone number and entered it in the address book of my phone, because I was beginning to like Philip, and I had an idea, which was to pick him up on our way down to the beach one day. What I was thinking was this: that Diddley and Dylan would make an excellent couple out in the dunes together, which they did, although as a threesome the canine gang did not make for the best of traveling companions. Diddley flew up from the back of the station wagon and over on to the backseat and then over on to Philip's lap in the front seat within seconds of his arrival. But only because Ollie beat him up as soon as he entered his personal space. This shenanigan provoked Dylan to compete. The method he chose was to put on an Olympic-standard performance of in-car gymnastics. The car rocked from side to side as if it were rehearsing to be a stage carriage in an amateur dramatical performance of *The Grapes of Wrath*. Thirty fraught minutes later out at Winterton-on-Sea, we made an entrance, of sorts: Diddley trying to break out of the sun roof, Dylan singing "Three Wheels on My Wagon," and Ollie's prehistoric frame rubbing against the steamed-up windows. We were the kind of toughs who could arrive at a beach parking lot feeling confident that no gang of bucket- and spade-wielding holiday-makers would mess with us. And that was just the dogs. Philip certainly looks the part. Handsome enough from ten paces, in close-up he is rough as a badger's arse, and I do not brush up much better.

In fact, and in contrast to the inner fantasy life I was building whereby I rode in the Wild West with Jesse James, the general public approached us readily because the first thing they saw was not a pair of hoods accompanied by three wild animals—no, the first thing they saw was a Dalmatian. My advice to any politician in need of a dose of positive publicity would be to adopt a Dalmatian. They are not even all that uncommon anymore, but the first words that 99 percent of people will say upon setting eyes on one is, "Ooh look! A Dalmatian!" It's almost an automatic human response; Dalmatians are the first-snowfall-of-winter of dog breeds.

While making our way through the dunes, we met a man who was walking along with a pronounced limp. It was this malingerer who set Philip off on a retelling of the "trouble last time" episode. The conclusion to the trouble last time (once again provoked by the activities of drug dealers) was that one of the several cops

Diddley: public relations expert.

who had turned up—one of the several who had been whacked by Philip in the course of restraining him—had threatened to sue him for damages for the time he might have to take off work due to a back injury that our hero was supposed to have caused. "I told him to eff off," Philip said. He went on to say that he'd further commented to the officer: "If you want a few days off work, take a couple of sick days like anyone else."

"*Did* you hurt him, though?" I asked.

"It was nothing, boy," he said.

"How many of them did you hit?" I asked. I had never quite worked it out during any of the previous versions.

Philip counted on his fingers. "All of them," he said.

The only thing I know about this side of life is what I've seen on television and in the movies. And I know what happens next. So I said: "I suppose you earned yourself a good kicking for that?"

"Oh yes, boy. They sorted me out in the cells all right."

He mimed a demonstration, one in which his arms were behind his back once again, but this time they were forced up and twisted while he was receiving the toe-end of the size nines in the rear joints of his knees. Some months later, Philip was trying to get into volunteer work, helping young offenders, individuals who were headed along the same road he had gone down. His reckoning was that he was exactly the sort of person— indeed the only sort of person—that might have a chance of influencing them, because he at least knew the score, which "most of 'em don't have a clue, boy," by which he meant the social workers. On the application for the volunteer work, and as part of his ongoing "self-help therapy"—which was essentially a policy of openness and honesty—Philip had come clean about his record. He had twelve counts of assaulting police officers to his name. Perhaps he had always been rather too honest in expressing his feelings; maybe this was one of his difficulties, and maybe this was something that attracted me to him: the job description of "writing" is to modulate experience through language. This is a secondhand, vicarious activity, one that benefits from the distancing cloak of cool consideration; writing is the exact opposite of the outbursts of unmediated emotion that Philip so often described to me. He certainly let his true feelings be known when confronted by the law, that was for sure. No doubt the Norfolk constabulary were well aware of him and took a grim view of his violent tendencies, tendencies you would never guess at out here in Winterton-on-Sea. Philip cupped his hand to light a cigarette and looked on indulgently as Dylan rolled Diddley, attempting to have sex with him from behind. Meanwhile, Ollie lay in the sand minding his own business and warming his belly. This is the most relaxed you will ever see Ollie. He loves sand. "They're right enjoying themselves, aren't they," Philip said. He smiled. "Thanks for bringing us out here, that's just what I need. I ain't been to the beach for years, boy."

I looked at him. What is he doing with a Dalmatian? I suddenly thought. Most men with his résumé would choose a Staffordshire bull terrier, a Rottweiler, or a specifically mated crossbreed selected from one of these types as their "statement of intent." They do not keep them as pets, they keep them as accessories to their gangsta lifestyles.

Some time later Philip was telling me another of his stories, this one concerning a brawl that took place between himself and a well-known family of four brothers. The venue for this incident was one of the many pubs from which he had subsequently been banned. (He struggles to remember whether certain of these bans have expired or not. The most inconveniencing was from his local, which excluded him from the third point of his Bermuda Triangle: bookies–pub–flat. He repeatedly popped into this local to inquire whether the ban had expired until, I imagine in complete exasperation, the landlord said, "Yes, it has." It must be easier to know where Philip is, safe at the bar, rather than to put up with the daily pestering from the threshold.) The telling detail in the episode concerning the encounter with the four brothers was that one of them threatened to punch Philip with a fist on which each finger, and also the thumb, was accessorized by a collection of sovereign rings.

"That's playing dirty, isn't it though," he said, in an

expression of proper disgust. "It's like using a knuckle duster."

"Dishonorable," I said.

"Exactly, boy," he replied. "Kid stuff."

This anecdote was the illustration of an attitude. If you are the genuine article, you can keep any dog you like, because the dog is for companionship, not for protection. You can take care of that part yourself.

The Guardian Angel

Elsewhere, though, someone had been increasingly taking on the mantle of "tough" on behalf of Dylan. The matter of his acceptance as the new arrival was complete now, and it was here that some slightly cockeyed instinct began to take hold in Ollie. He would steam in as soon as any other animal approached, to ensure that everything was safe. More than nine times out of ten this intervention was unnecessary, and on the tenth time it was not usually required either. What began as a mildly irritating habit developed into a syndrome, which ultimately escalated into a problem.

Ollie began compiling a list of "Dogs I Do Not Like" when he was very young. It started with a Belgian shepherd, one that bit him on the backside. Ollie was asking for it, on that occasion, by trying to provoke a playful run out of an animal who was clearly a miserable old sod by sledging the back of the Belgian shepherd's neck. His technique for dealing with any future Belgian shepherd, or German shepherd (he grouped them together), was to give a wide berth. I thought his approach slightly meek, but Ollie had such a vast range of psychological problems when he was a juvenile that this matter really was the least of my concerns. To all shepherd-type dogs, and any dog that looked a bit like one, he later added all boxers after two set upon him at once, forcing him to put his fangs out to full effect. Fair enough.

But once Dylan came along and had been accepted into Ollie World, the list of those to whom he took exception extended rapidly, alarmingly, and exponentially. Labradors and retrievers (except those that were already his friends), spaniels, Border collies, anything big and brown like an Airedale, anything big and black like a giant poodle, anything big and red (with the exception of Rhodesian ridgebacks): all of these joined the roll call of breeds that he was likely to "front up" in an increasingly menacing manner. Growling, the hairs of his back standing on end, the display of a full set of teeth. This was Ollie saying, "Go ahead, punk, make my day." In short, he was becoming aggressive. I told him off for it, of course, and encouraged him to behave otherwise by using the expression: "Ollie, *be nice*."

This was useless.

After catching ahold of his collar and apologizing to the other owner with words to the effect that he was "going through a funny spell," I'd have a further message for him.

"Look at Dylan," I'd say. "Not only are you frightening him, but you're holding him back: can't you see he'd actually like to play with that dog you've just brutalized?"

This was also useless. Ollie doesn't understand English, as it is not even his first language (which is an arcane Egyptian-Romany dialect). But, and moreover, I could see that whatever *my* stated view was, *his* was that he was only doing his job, the job of protecting our family group from attack (by Labradors). He was sorry, but in this instance, as in so many others, he was right, and I was wrong. When he went out with Trezza it was even worse. He knows which gender his owners are, and he put extra effort into protecting the fairer sex.

His health was generally excellent; it was a good while since we had had cause to rush him to the pet hospital because he had collided with a vehicle, or because he had stuck his head into a wasp nest so that his face erupted into a fistful of stings, looking like a pound of raspberries, or because he had eaten a doughnut and got the runs plus vomiting. In short, he had been quiet for too long. Something had to give, and here it was: the maniac streak was back. The variety of Guardian Angel he went in for was not, of course, the benign spirit who guides you across the road in the nick of time before the hammer falls from the scaffolding to cave your head in; rather it was the type who is the founding member of a sect of vigilantes, those who take it upon themselves to patrol the subways of New York City at night. Ollie had become hard.

The Incident of the
Kite in the Field

B ut Ollie was not yet—and neither, even once he'd started, was he always—in vigilante mode. He indulged himself in peaceful passages of behavior, allowing periods of time for young Dylan to express his own personality and bring it to the fore. We were walking along, man and his dogs, minding our own business, early one breezy evening when Dylan saw his first kite. This was at the university, on the sports fields. The way these fields are set up is that three are laid out end to end in a long flat plain, while a fourth is situated higher up a bank on a plateau. The kite flyer was flying his kite on the higher field.

He was obscured from our view by the bank, though this was not the case with the kite. On catching sight of it, Dylan reared up on his hind legs and howled like a wolf. By now, his voice was in the process of breaking, rendering his wolf-like howling thoroughly convincing.

He bounced two steps forward, toward the kite, still on his hind legs, while continuing to howl with extra fortissimo.

He bounced one step back, reverse-howling.

"Dylan, dear boy, calm down," I said, with all the authority, and all the net effect, of Captain Mainwaring issuing a command. "It's only a kite," I said.

"No, Master," his body language replied. "It's a pterodactyl. They are deadly, but I will kill it for you, because that is my Saluki duty, even if the truth of the matter is that I find it pretty terrifying."

He continued to bounce back and forth until he was up close to the kite flyer. Here he assumed the semi-prone position: front legs stretched out, head on the ground, chin pointing up, arse in the air. From the relative safety of this pose he proceeded to bark at the kite flyer for all he was worth, interspersing the din with interludes of the bouncing back and forth and the reverse-howling. Could the man not see the danger he was in!?

This did not look good, and indeed it wasn't good. I ran toward Dylan with the intention of clearing him out of the way of the kite flyer, who, I assumed, would be hacked off. In fact, he was not hacked off at all. He was so absorbed in his activity (the kite was one of those large steerable contraptions, like a sail) that he was paying scant, if any, attention to Dylan's contribution.

Eventually, and nothing to do with me, Dylan decided that enough terror was enough and tore off to hide in some trees five hundred yards away. Ollie, who has

See 'em off, boy (to achieve this shot, simply hold a kite aloft).

never noticed a kite in the five years he has been with us, adopted a statue-like pose while he observed all of this. Once Dylan had cleared the area, he took matters into his own hands. In Dylan's absence, he ran up at the kite flyer and took over on barking duty. He never, ever barks at anyone, it's just not done. But, having started this new trick, he decided to stick at it.

Woof: It was you, wasn't it? *Woof*: It was you who scared my kid brother. *Woof woof*: Watch it, boy. *Woof woof woof*: Or you'll have me to deal with in the future. *Woof woof woof woof*: Understood?

The kite flyer turned around. "Sorry," I said, the least I *could* say, considering I seemed to have not one, but two, out-of-control animals with me. Certain kite flyers, I discovered at that point, share the worldview of surf bums. He was a young man with scruffy facial hair, one who just shrugged and smiled as if to say: "Animals, they're far out, aren't they, dude?"

Ollie suddenly stopped his barking and ran off into a copse of trees five hundred yards away and on the other side of the field to those that Dylan was in. Now I found myself in the situation that I had feared at the outset: two of them on the missing list, in opposite directions. I had to be thankful for small mercies. At least I knew roughly where Dylan was from the continuing sound effects. He had spotted a squirrel up a tree and he had a great deal to say to him about his cheating, vertical habits. A mere half hour later I had Dylan returned to one leash and Ollie to the other. I walked toward the parking lot wondering if there wasn't some college into which I might enroll myself for classes in "Being a Master."

Dylan and the Fishmongers

I often treat myself on a Friday morning by driving the boys early to the beach. It's completely out of hours, by which I mean it's not the weekend, and we are more or less on our own. The Protestant work ethic means I attend to my desk on Saturday and Sunday, to make amends for the indulgence, even though I *am* an honorary Catholic (an ideal combination: a sense of guilt combined with a sense of duty).

The scent of the sea gets into me and, since it's a Friday, I make it my quasi-religious routine to buy fish and a crab for lunch on my way back. I used to get this from a van by the side of the road, but one particular Friday my attention was caught by a chalked sign outside a fishmongers on the east side of Norwich: *Cromer Crab, Fresh Today*. There was a hand-drawn picture of a crab to go with the information. I had passed the fishmongers many times, but something about the drawing of the crab made me pull up. The shop is on a corner. It has a low-rent old-fashioned charm: you enter through a screen of vertical chains, chains that remind me of the plastic ribbons that used to flutter across the entrance to the local chip shop when I was a boy. Plastic lobsters decorate the walls, which are tiled in white ceramic, floor to ceiling. As well as an assortment of fresh fish, they stock a few items that take you down memory lane, like those flat cans of anchovies that you open with a key. Their crab was excellent, more expensive, but much better than the crab from the van, so I transferred my allegiance and became a semi-regular client. The two ladies who serve are friendly enough. They are up for a certain amount of banter, but if a genuine local turns up you can spot the distinction between yourself and that individual right away. The truth of the matter is that it can take a while to be accepted in Norwich, say about twenty years on average.

Dylan and the Fishmongers

Owning a dog, I've discovered, speeds up this process; it was not until after Ollie came along that I could say I made friends with anyone who was born and bred in Norfolk. The first time I was invited into a local's home was as a consequence of Ollie, as a consequence of his fame, to be precise—we were asked over to sign a book. I had lived in the city for seventeen years by then, annexed off in an enclave that consisted exclusively of immigrants, in the ghetto of the professional middle classes. I had not started there; I was a painter and decorator when I arrived, a working-class regular. In that capacity I was treated politely yet regarded with suspicion by my fellow Norfolk and Norwich born-and-bred building-trade comrades. It was as if I were a foreigner, but of the type that is not wholly unacceptable. It was a bit like, say, being Spanish.

***

It was Good Friday morning. Philip texted me at eight, phoned me quarter past and then again at half past, this time leaving a message saying: When I had woken up, did I fancy a walk out with the dogs?

"Been up ages, boy," I texted him back from where I

sat reading the *Eastern Daily Press* and drinking tea in bed (it is these slovenly ways, too, that I seek to redress with the twin weapons of Protestant work ethic and quasi-Catholic guilt). Dylan was lying on my feet looking at me hopefully: crumbs have been known to fall his way from the early-morning biscuits. If you'd have told me a few years earlier that I'd have been happy to have a dog in bed with me I'd have told you in no uncertain terms that you'd got the wrong man. But even though my scale of what was—and what was not—acceptable regarding matters of personal hygiene had been radically revised once I'd taken to giving Ollie a goodnight kiss on each of his cheeks and his forehead, there was no way I would have allowed him onto our bed. But of course, once Dylan had found his way there early one morning and I had discovered that he made an excellent feet warmer, I modified this view: not only would it be cruel, it would be actively counterproductive to shove him off. I have revised my list of favorite smells, too, since he came along. They previously stood as follows:

1. New tires
2. The sandpaper on the side of a matchbox
3. Pipe smoke

4. Coffee
5. Old-fashioned linseed oil–based putty

Dylan's cheesy feet are to be added to that list, possibly replacing the putty. I often sniff his pads when he makes himself comfortable next to me on the sofa at night, stretching his legs toward my face while he naps. The smell is difficult to encapsulate in words. It is delicate, earthy, vaguely young-Camembert-like with a touch of very-old-book. It sounds repulsive, of course, but is not; like yesterday's wood shavings, it is rather complex in its aromatic subtlety.

***

Once I was out of my bed on this particular Friday morning, I picked Philip up at our usual meeting place, outside a branch of William Hill, and we proceeded on to the university. The previous week, Ollie had been put on the restricted-exercise list since he had required a couple of stitches after having had a small lump removed from his leg. So, for the first time in their history, the Guardian Angel was left behind and Dylan and Diddley were out playing together without

the presence of their chaperone. The weather was bit-
terly cold and windy, too. Each and every fellow dog
walker that we bumped into was suitably pious and
self-congratulatory.

"Only the hardcore out today!" This was the standard cheery greeting.

As Philip and I felt ourselves to be among the highest
echelon of this category (so hardcore that we didn't feel
any need to mention the conditions, while he even had
his shirt hanging out of his trousers), we decided to put
in an extra-long shift of walking in order to prove the
matter. We went over the fields, doubled back along the
river, and then went right around the far side of the lake.
All incident-free. Philip had observed that this was good
practice for Dylan, that it would enhance his sense of
maturity to be away from Ollie for once. I had a sense
of reservation about coming on to the land between the
nearside of the lake and the dorm buildings, as that area
was always slightly precautionary since it is known to
contain a surplus of rabbits. But it was the morning,
which was officially safe, as opposed to the evening,
which was officially code red. I had already had difficulties with him twice that week, on one occasion being
made to wait for twenty minutes up at the dunes at Win-

terton as night fell and he continued with his hunting. Up at the coast I had put the whistle into use. I had, by now, spent some time "whistle training" him in a stable. He was the world's fastest learner. The first time I blasted it he whirled around to look at me in his full-alert squirreling stance, his hair standing on end and his tail perpendicular. What the hell was that? I stood holding a piece of slightly warm steak in my hand (I had it in tinfoil in my pocket: the stable is not far from our house). Dylan was in like Flynn. Within five minutes I could pull him in any direction I wanted using the combination of steak and a whistle. I repeated the exercise every day for two weeks. Perfect: he was trained to complete obedience. Up at the beach I had discovered that this applied only so long as he was in a stable, with no distractions. If rabbits were introduced to the equation, his response to this "training" was precisely nil.

Up at the beach I was quietly furious. You cannot easily spot a dog in sand dunes under a blackening sky: I was powerless to do anything but occasionally reblast the whistle (it might at least frighten off bad men who lurk in the dark) and wait. I walked toward the parking lot, hoping that, wherever he was, he might at least see this and follow me. He did not.

Eventually I ventured back into the cold, dark dunes in order to keep my circulation going. Suddenly, and entirely by chance, Dylan happened my way, doing his best to look the least bit sheepish:

"Ah, there you are at last, Master; I *was wondering* where you had gone off to . . ."

***

Now, as we entered the slightly risky arena in front of the lake, I glanced back to Dylan. He seemed to be engrossed in his continued skirmish with Diddley. He seemed safe enough. I looked around again twenty seconds later. He had galloped over to the far side of the field near a dirt track that tradesmen's vans use in the service of the never-ending task of refurbishing and extending the university buildings. Beyond the track lie the dorms, the whole campus, and the majority rabbit population. I blew on the whistle. Dylan looked back at me, practically stuck his middle finger up, dropped his nose to the ground, and went on his way for a damn good truffle.

"He did that deliberately all right, boy," said Philip, helpfully.

"I should have put him on the leash before we got here," I said. "It's my fault."

In a flash, he was nowhere in sight, a situation I was beginning to feel I was experiencing much too often of late. Five minutes elapsed. Ten minutes elapsed. It remained bitter, a little hail fell. Philip went up around the far side to see if there was any sight of him. I remained where I was, occasionally blowing the whistle, to absolutely no effect whatsoever. After thirteen minutes Dylan reappeared, flying toward me like a train, the little sod. But on the other hand he was here, still in one piece, and at least having the wit to make a pretense of being a good boy who was making his way back to his master. He cornered hard as he passed within ten feet of me, gave me a wide berth, and continued his journey on up to Philip and Diddley. Treacherous. He passed those two by the same ten-foot margin and disappeared once more behind a different dorm building.

"At least he's checking up on where you are, boy," said Philip.

"You wouldn't exactly describe it as obedience though, would you?" I replied.

"To be honest, boy, no."

The campus was deserted, it was like Christmas Eve.

All the same I counted the movement of five cars in the time that Dylan was out of sight. It was this that I was really worried about.

In his own good time, he finally reappeared, a further thirteen minutes since the last sighting. Diddley, bored with all the waiting around, had distracted himself by digging a large hole. He took his head out of the hole and looked at Dylan as he headed across toward the Sainsbury Centre for Visual Arts, and then he looked at me. He hasn't finished yet, mate, he seemed to say. He stuck his head back down the hole.

Thirty cold, bitter, windy minutes after he'd started this game, Dylan finally came back within range. Usually, at this point, he will become a dog again, as opposed to a wild, savage hunter. He will take a treat from the hand, and that in turn means we can take his collar, attach him to the leash, resist the urge to kick him on the backside, and be on our way. This time he came within range as usual but then he took it upon himself to dance backward at every offer of food. This time he was extending the activity into the next logical stage: advanced disobedience. This time he was not for being caught.

We met a family group, out for their Good Friday constitutional. "What sort of breed is that?" the man of the group asked of Dylan. "We've been watching him: is he some sort of field dog?"

"He is some sort of exceptionally disobedient dog," I replied. "If by any chance he comes near, you couldn't grab hold of his collar for me, could you?"

Dylan more than went near, he went into their very midst. The man reached down toward him, which allowed Dylan an opportunity to demonstrate his expertise at jumping four feet backward from a standing start. Even finding himself within a group of people he did not know, people who might at least be expected to benefit from the element of surprise when it came to the matter of his liberty, he remained on red alert. He skirted the evil family group of dogcatchers, which put him within reach of Philip.

"C'mon, Dylan, boy," Philip said. He lowered his hand, offering the treat, and nearly, but not quite, collaring him. As Dylan shot backward, Philip completed his failed attempt with a lunging rugby dive that landed him facedown in the mud, while a fresh flurry of hail billowed up the back of his shirt. "The little bastard," he said.

It was fifteen minutes—and several more Dylan-solo excursions into assorted woods later—before he finally remembered that he was supposed to be a domestic dog and that he had arrived here earlier with friends. He suddenly cantered back into our pack as if nothing had happened. The whole episode had lasted three-quarters of an hour, though it seemed longer.

"What are you gonna do about him, boy?" Philip asked.

The answer to this was that I did not know. The obvious and safe thing would be never to let him loose, but you can't do that with an animal who is born to run.

I piled them all back in the car and, remembering it was a Friday, went to pick up my regular crab from the new regular fishmongers.

"Still cold out, is it?" asked the woman behind the counter.

"Yes," I replied, "especially if you've just spent three-quarters of an hour in a field trying to get hold of a dog."

"Oh," she said, "what sort of dog?"

I indicated through the window. "The one staring out the back of that car across the road."

"The one that looks as though butter wouldn't melt," she said.

"That's him."

"A Saluki," she said.

Not many people can identify the breed at that distance with just the head to go by. I nodded.

"Well, that's why then," she said. "Nothing to be done about it. They just do whatever the hell they like, don't they."

I didn't need to ask her whether she had ever owned one: she'd confirmed as much by stating this truism. She went into the rear of the shop and returned with a bag of fish heads, a treat to reward Dylan for his excellent conduct. She invited herself outside to take a closer look. This was a lot more friendly than I had any right to expect without patronizing the establishment for several more years yet. I opened the tailgate. "Aren't you lovely," she said to Dylan as he dabbed his wet nose into the palms of her beautiful, fish-scented hands. "Yes, and you're lovely, too," she said to Diddley, who had moved forward to demand his rightful share of the fuss.

"That'll encourage him to behave then, boy," Philip said as we drove away to pick up a couple of long-overdue espressos and a slice of chocolate cheesecake to take back for Jayne, Philip's girlfriend. "Now he knows he gets a bag of cod cheeks out of it, he'll certainly never do that again."

Good point.

And, sorry to say, the long Good Friday episode was nothing compared to what happened one night out at the dunes a few weeks later, henceforth to be known as the epic.

The Epic

Though, in a sense, it was possible to predict the epic, it was, in an equal sense, impossible to predict it, too. It took place on a Tuesday evening. On the Saturday before—just three nights earlier—we had had a quiet hour up at the beach, more or less incident-free. Prior to this Saturday walk I had sat in the car anxiously awaiting the final soccer scores. It was the sixth-last game of the season: Stoke had drawn away to Sheffield on Wednesday, which left us in the second automatic promotion place. This was completely uncharted water; we had not been in the top flight for twenty-three years and now we were only five matches away from it. I thought about it a lot on the walk; I had awkward and compromised emotions to deal with because I had developed a deep loathing for the manager who was about to achieve this miracle. He was a long-ball merchant who was one-dimensional in every regard. Watching the type of game he served up was a complete waste of my time: there was more aesthetic beauty in a minute of Dylan's running than in a season of Pulis's games. *But*: this year it was beginning to look as though his tactics might possibly bear fruit in the form of promotion. I had to separate my personal feelings of animosity for Pulis from my lifelong support of my hometown team. I walked along alternately grinding my teeth and dreaming of the happy future where our team had made it to the EPL. After the walk I drove home and then took a dish of sea bass around to friends for dinner, with fish purchased earlier in the day from my new favorite fishmongers. The reason their crab was twice the price of the crab that I had been buying from the van at the side of the road, they told me, was that *they* dressed their own, whereas the van man most likely didn't (now that we had established a full relationship, and Dylan had cod cheeks sent out for him on a regular

basis, I was privy to all sorts of inside information).
The fishmonger himself pulled the claws back from a
crab and showed me. All that would contain once he
had dressed it was what I was looking at now, see, meat
that had originally come from this very shell, unlike the
cheaper varieties where every bit of flesh is mechani-
cally recovered and only a little white meat ends up in
each of the "shells," which are not shells but are made
out of plastic and which are *smaller*. There's a factory
where this takes place, up near the coast, where they
buy everything from the catch and chuck it all into the
machines: crabs with only one claw, a couple of stray
prawns, whatever they find. That is what you end up
with on your plate, unlike in this establishment where
everything is premium, or at least as premium as is possible in this day and age.

In between the Saturday evening of the lovely bass
and the epic Tuesday night that was to follow—on the
Monday morning—we had gone up there en famille,
which is unusual: whereas I regard the beach as a daily
fact of life, Trezza sees it as something of an excursion.
In addition to the excursion aspect, which takes time
and involves the preparation of a flask and everything,
Trezza avoids going out with me all that often in any

case because my walking style is incorrect. My normal pace is practically a march, which annoys her. In this she is not alone. Philip has complained about it ("Just stopping to roll a smoke now, boy," he will shout, as I press on, "if you don't mind"), and Toby, the old friend who advised me that a new pup would demolish the kitchen, has complained about it, too: "Hold on, is this some sort of race?" Toby asked. "And why are we walking like this when we had three bottles of wine last night, too?" he went on. (To atone, of course.)

I go too fast, I accept it, but it *is* my natural speed, and just for the record it's as much of a nuisance for faster walkers like me to drag along like a tortoise as it is for slow amblers to get a bit of a move on.

But anyway, this Monday was a beautiful, sunny morning, we had a beautiful, slow-paced walk, and there was the thermos of coffee waiting for us back in the car on our return, too. Whenever I think of my old Uncle Joe, the driest uncle of my schoolboy days, I picture a tartan thermos, a battered station wagon, and some homemade fish-paste sandwiches. Our flask may be finished in stainless steel, and there are no paste sandwiches, but otherwise I had become like old Uncle Joe. I was no longer any sort of rock'n'roller, no matter whether Keith Richards kept a pair of dogs down in his mansion in Turks and Caicos or not.

***

Thirty-six hours later I was back at Winterton-on-Sea. It was a quiet drive out. The thought crossed my mind that Dylan was maturing: his singing, which after all was only a signal of immature impatience, seemed to be decreasing in both quantity and volume. The wind was up when we arrived; a fine sandstorm blew low across the surface of the beach, which seemed to provoke the boys into a more-than-usual amount of skittishness. The sand must have been getting into Dylan's eyes, I think. This is how it started. Halfway into the outward-bound leg, from the beachside, he dived up and away into the dunes. It's not unusual, that, but I don't like it because he gets his nose down into the crack cocaine of the rabbits and then . . . Well, we already know what that can lead to. The organizing principle, the technique, that he employed when he went off on the hunt was one I had come to recognize. Although he was busy, he kept us in his orbit, or rather his radius: he repeatedly, albeit at longer intervals than I'd prefer, checked up on our whereabouts before darting back to the epicenter of activity. By these means, I would at least occasionally catch sight of him. There would be no hope of recall at this stage, but on the other hand he was not running off for miles in a straight line either, an option that, while clearly within his capacity, was not within his mind.

Ollie played no part in the rabbiting—he is past it, it holds no interest for him, not unless one of them is dim enough to walk right under his nose, in which case he is forced into a desultory pursuit. Instead, he tracks alongside me. I throw him the occasional small, round biscuit from among the treats in my pocket: he prefers to chase biscuits along the sand than rabbits. Biscuits are easier to catch.

I look up to where Dylan was last seen. Ollie stops to look, too. "Yes, where has the little devil gone, anyway?" he seems to be saying. "He's a pest, isn't he," he seems also to be saying. "But as I've mentioned all too often in the past, you've only yourself to blame for bringing him into the family in the first place, haven't you."

On this occasion, though, I noted a slight urgency about Ollie's glances toward where his brother was last sighted. He looked to the dunes, he looked to me, he looked to the dunes, he looked to me. There was no sign of Dylan at all. Ollie seemed to be implying something, and though I could not make a certain and accurate interpretation of what this was, he seemed to be saying: "I've got a funny feeling about this one, Master, watch out."

We made it to the hippie Maypole, the midpoint. For half the length—and half the time—of our walk, now, we had not seen Dylan. He was not employing his usual orbit/radius technique. I had yet to sound the whistle. Experience had taught me that it was, in any event, meaningless when pitted against rabbits, so it was best to use it judiciously, otherwise you just stood about parping away and looking like a fool. I climbed the highest dune and scanned every horizon. Nothing. A couple of birds, and that was it. I felt vaguely pissed off. This was the juvenile Ollie—who now stood sentry beside me—all over again. Any notion I might be entertaining to the effect that I exercised control over Dylan—who had known me from a pup, and who had none of the fear-psychosis that characterized Ollie during the long, awful period in his early days when he refused to return because he had become frightened of me—was, in these increasingly regular moments, revealed as self-deception. *Fuck you; I do what I want.* That was Dylan's motto.

I blew the damn whistle. More nothing. I sensed a movement behind me. Dylan had emerged from the lower slopes, north of the highest dune, from, as it were, farther away than we actually go. I called his name; he half glanced my way. Otherwise he kept his nose to the ground as he swung off with a low, cunning, quick, and stealthy action on another oblique tangent. Was it the same long trail, or many shorter, different trails that he was following? I didn't know, but whichever it was, it was much more important than me or Ollie. Ollie, having noted my movement toward Dylan, found that this gave him the clue to catch sight of his brother himself.

"Hey, Master, there he is!"

"Yes, Ollie, well done, boy."

He is no detective, that's for sure, and he had no instinct to set off and round him up on my behalf either, more to the point. Had he so wished, he could have grounded Dylan, he could have pinned him to the deck until I got there, he could have given me a genuine helping hand. None of this crossed Ollie's mind, of course. But though he was of little specific help, his sanguine presence gave me great comfort in the difficult times that lay in our immediate future.

The walk back to where I had parked the car—at

the top of the road that terminates at the beach head—afforded several more "at distance" sightings. There are many routes through those dunes; the one I was taking was being dictated by a combination of the sightings and the necessity of keeping to the highest ground in order that the sightings might continue. There was something of a military exercise about this; natural marching pace or not, I didn't need to be sent over all the roughest terrain as well. My feelings of irritation were escalating. We were nearing the end of our "jaunt," the "pleasure" of which had been severely diminished, since for three-quarters of an hour it was me who was being taken for a ride.

About four hundred yards from the parking lot, a tall warning sign juts out of the highest peak where the dunes join the beach. Dylan was on one of his longest stretches of "being out of sight," so in the interests of securing the best possible lookout position, I climbed up beside the sign. From here there was no sight of Dylan. This was Ollie's cue to put in an Oscar-winning performance of "being a model citizen." He came and sat solemnly beside me, where he wore an expression of suitable concern. The clocks had gone forward the previous weekend. As usual, this had taken me by surprise.

In theory, the arrival of British Summer Time was good news for me because it extended the amount of hours available for doing stuff. Like this. It had turned seven o'clock and it was still reasonably light. The sky was striking, drifting through several limpid shades of dirty dishwater; you could feel the season changing. I meditated on the notes of the sky for a while as all around me nothing continued to happen. Suddenly, Dylan appeared a hundred yards north on the long serrated dune that divides the beach from the scrub. I whistled at him; he disappeared. I knelt down and tickled Ollie behind the ears. "He's a little bastard, isn't he," I said to him. I stood, surveying. A couple had come into sight, approaching from the direction of the village. As they neared I could see that they were accompanied by a pair of dogs. Ollie flirted down. I hoped he wasn't going to come over all Guardian Angel, I had enough trouble on my plate as it was. But no, he kept up his model citizen act. He let things be, even though both dogs were potential "trouble," one being a Labrador, the other a black spaniel. I explained to the couple what I was doing, standing there in a silent, vigilant, and weird way.

"I've got one on the missing list," I said.

"Oh," said the man. "Is that normal?"

That was a question that clearly came from an experienced dog owner. "Sort of," I replied. "Increasingly so," I said. "He's a youngster," I said, by way of putting the case for the defense. "The rabbits make him mental," I concluded.

"We used to have a lot of trouble with her," he said, nodding at the Labrador, "always running off with other dogs, and not coming back."

"We got her a collar . . ." the woman said.

". . . one of those that zap them." The man finished the sentence for her.

"Did it work?" I asked.

The couple indicated the obedient animal beside them: the living proof that, yes, it did indeed work. They went on to explain that the collar delivers a small buzz, or electric shock, from a handheld device, and a noise, too, and that after a while, as the behavior improves, you deactivate the shock part of it and just have the noise.

"The animal-rights groups don't like them," the man said.

"Why not?" I asked, an indication of how distracted I was because the answer to that was obvious.

"There's one that emits just a smell that animals don't

like . . . lemon or something. That one *is* approved," the woman said.

"But that one doesn't work," the man said.

I hadn't kept up with any of this "deterrent collar" technology or debate, but right now I'd have been happy with one that pinned Dylan to the ground by staple-gunning a set of cocktail sticks through his pelt to hold him to the floor like a cartoon cat spread-eagled to a dartboard. I contented myself with saying to the couple that I would seriously think about getting one of their recommended collars should it be the case that I ever got him to return. At this moment the dog in question made a guest appearance, this time only fifty yards away, once more down the way on the long straight dune north.

"Ah, is that him?" the couple asked.

"It is," I replied.

"How old is he, exactly?" the man said.

"Eighteen months."

"Ah," he said, "the peak of teenage naughtiness. And I see he's no slouch either."

"He sort of blends in to the background, doesn't he," the woman added. "That can't help."

They'd got the picture all right.

***

I followed the couple down to the beach. The appearance of their two dogs, with whom Ollie was now happily playing, gave rise to a little hope insofar as capture went. Dylan *must* come forward to investigate this turn of events, surely. And so he did. Some skittish skirmishing took place. I ought to be able to get in among this and offer him a treat while collaring him. The moment my hand went down he sprang back as if he had hit an electric fence.

"Ah," said the woman.

"He's done this before," I said, "and quite recently, too: it's new."

"What great sport," she said.

"Exactly," her husband replied as he watched. "He thinks that's tremendous fun, doesn't he?"

The woman and her husband separated themselves from each other by forty yards or so. He wandered around with the Lab, and each time Dylan came near he tried to tempt him in with his own treats. He had the element of surprise that I had lost, but all the same Dylan knew exactly what his game was. Dylan finessed his technique at jumping backward from a standing start over the next thirty minutes, as each of these two kind individuals dedicated themselves to helping me out. As the light of the day fell away over the horizon, I stood completely still. There was nothing I could do to help. At one point I could feel the man hold his breath as the woman, who remained crouching on the sand, almost had him. Dylan allowed her hand to come within an inch of his neck before he powered backward as if he were taking off from Cape Canaveral. And then he gave up on the pretense that he might allow either of these two to nearly catch him. Instead he loped away, back up to the dunes.

"Oh no," said the woman. "What are you going to do now?"

I really didn't know.

In addition to the imminent darkness, which was only minutes away, it was beginning to get cold. Ollie sat on the sand, shivering slightly. I thanked the couple for their efforts, which I considered well beyond the call of duty, and I walked away. It was five to eight. I took the cell phone out of my jacket pocket and checked in with base, saying it might be a good idea to put tinfoil over my dinner. Trezza was suitably appalled by my story and advised "going back up to the car with Ollie and seeing what happens."

"What's he doing now?" she asked.

What he was doing now was running several hundred yards down the beach to the tide's edge, where three bodies were silhouetted against the horizon. They were huddled around a single fishing rod that pointed out to sea.

"He's gone off to annoy some fishermen," I said.

"Stay calm," Trezza advised. "You're doing well," she said. "Hang in there," she said. It was like Ground Control to Captain Kirk.

Just when you thought it couldn't get much worse, there was still an opportunity for a slight deterioration. Dylan kicked in with the howling-like-a-wolf routine. At the fishermen. Ordinarily, fishermen tend not to roll out the red carpet for dogs. The very least that a boisterous young animal is likely to do is attempt to eat their maggots. Two out of the three fishermen began jumping at Dylan, to see him off. Fair enough, I thought, though it was hardly going to help me insofar as catching ahold of him was concerned. It would just pile wariness onto the disobedience. I took Trezza's advice and walked up the dunes to the car. Ollie stayed put, sitting on the sand and looking somewhat apprehensive about the whole situation. Eventually, he gave up on this and, ever so slowly, adopting the style of a creaky old man, he made his way up to join me. I let him into the back of the station wagon. By now, Dylan had run away from the fishermen and was nowhere to be seen. It was dark. I stood by the car using my remaining useful sense: listening. A dog's ID tag rattles against the collar. That is what I was listening for. I could hear nothing. I suffered a moment of existential angst. What the hell was I doing? I ought to be having a totally cool life, living in a loft in downtown New York City and dating Jennifer Aniston, not standing here being royally fucked about. After about ten minutes, two of the "fishermen" came up toward me. I wondered what it was they would have to say vis-à-vis matters related to dog control. Nothing, as it turned out. They were teenage boys who had simply been passing time with the third guy, the one who remained down there, the actual fisherman. Our family moved to the Isle of Man for nearly a year when I was a teenager. The Isle of Man appears to be almost all coast; I recognized what these boys had been doing immediately: they had been finding ways of entertaining themselves under the handicap of living out here in the middle of nowhere. (The whole of the Isle of Man was the middle of nowhere, so far as we were concerned.)

"You haven't seen a dog anywhere, have you?" I asked them.

"The gray one?"

"Yes," I said.

"Oh, is he yours, mister?"

It was a genuine question, and one that required an answer. "Yes," I said. "I've been trying to catch him for more than an hour now."

"Oh," they said. "That's no good. We'll go try and find him for you. What's his name?"

"Dylan," I replied.

The two boys ran back down to the beach and headed off in opposite directions, calling out, "Dylan. Dylan! *Dylan!*"

Though it was my view that they hadn't a hope, I felt enormous gratitude to them. I had only been alone for a short while after the couple had gone; now, once more, I had allies. Do not knock the youth of today, I thought. They're all right. I watched the boys conduct their search for another seven or eight minutes while I thought about the lights of Manhattan and Jennifer Aniston's shining hair; would she *really* have even gone to the airport to get the plane to Paris at the end of the series if she were dating me instead of that Ross bloke?

I doubted it. Suddenly, I imagined I heard something. Actually, it was not my imagination; there was a definite tinkling coming from the far side of the dunes, from the southeast, to the right, from the direction in which we never go. It sounded as if something was going on. It sounded like more than one dog.

Dylan came first, just ahead of a greyhound with whom he was larking. The greyhound was wearing a red jacket. Behind the greyhound was an older white-haired woman in a long coat and sneakers. "Hello," she called.

"Hello," I replied.

"I thought I recognized that dog," she said.

I knew her only vaguely: we had bumped into each other once or twice over the preceding winter.

"I don't suppose you could put your hand on his collar for me, could you?" I said.

She made an unforced effort from just behind. Dylan flirted away, easy. I remembered the teenage boys and shouted down to them. They ran back. They arrived at the top of the beach road together with the older woman, Dylan, and the greyhound, the whole ensemble suddenly forming a loose pack. The two boys had a go apiece at catching Dylan's collar; each time he flirted away. "Best leave him," I said. "It'll only make him worse."

I brought the woman up to speed with the situation.

"An hour and a half?" she said. "That *is* a long time. Do you think if you started the car engine he would come to you?"

I said I didn't think that would make any difference. I said I was pretty sure that one car engine would sound the same as the next to Dylan.

"Where do you live?" I asked.

"In the village," she replied.

That, I considered good news. Dylan was very interested in her greyhound, who was named Luke, and he remained quite close to him, looking for fun. I asked the woman her name, which was Elizabeth. I thought it likely that Dylan would follow Luke and Elizabeth home, and that then he would be trapped within the walls of a garden, or the house itself, and that then I would have him. All we had to do now was all walk casually into the village, without any more rabbits showing up in the dunes that line the road back down there, a route of a quarter-mile or so, and that would be the end of it. I could even drive, light the way with the headlights. I looked to the car. The tailgate of the station wagon was open. Something in there suddenly caught Dylan's attention.

"Oh," he seemed to say. "Look, everybody! There's Ollie!"

And he jumped in to greet him. And I closed the door behind. I felt a huge relief. I had been thinking about Jennifer Aniston as a way of not thinking about having to stay out there all night—as if even *that* would have worked, as if even a long, long wait would have delivered a result (because by then Dylan could be ten miles away).

He didn't lie down in the back of the car so much as he collapsed. He was very, very tired indeed. Ollie, who I thought might have treated him to at least a mild duffing, also seemed relieved to be reunited with the irritant. He simply lay down behind him. They were practically spooning; they were a picture of pastoral repose.

"They're so beautiful," said Elizabeth. "But what will you *do*. About Dylan?"

"Right now I feel like giving him a damn good kick up the backside . . ."

Elizabeth's face crumpled.

". . . Of course I would never do that," I reassured

her. "But really, Elizabeth," I said, "I feel like I never want to let him off the leash again."

Her face crumpled once more. "Oh no, you mustn't," she said. "These animals are born to be free and to run. Not that *he's* badly behaved," she said, meaning her own dog. "You're a very good boy, aren't you, Luke."

She went on to mention that it was just as well that Luke was no trouble because she had only had him for a few months, since her husband passed away about a year ago, and that she wouldn't have been able to manage a difficult animal.

"I forget where things are, you know," she said. "Do you do that?"

"All the time," I said, both to offer her comfort in her condition, whatever it was, and also because it was true. Perhaps her forgetfulness explained why it was that she was walking out here in the dunes in the dark.

"I had a lot of trouble with him, too," I said, nodding at Ollie, in a slightly misjudged effort to distract attention away from Dylan's behavior.

"Is he a rescue?" she asked.

"Mmm-hmm," I said. "In fact," I added, "I had so much trouble with him I wrote a book about it."

"Oh," she said. "Did it do well?"

"Not too badly," I replied.

"Well, that's that then," she said. "You were meant to be together."

I don't believe in that sort of mumbo jumbo, but I was tired by now. I was tired, cold, worn out, fed up, pissed off, and very relieved. That, I discovered, is the perfect combination of energies to get you believing in mumbo jumbo. "I suppose we were," I said.

I climbed into the car and turned the key and let the radiator begin to warm. It entered my mind that I ought to have worried about Elizabeth walking home, but by the time I had got around to having this thought she was gone, disappeared back into the dunes. Maybe she was a ghost, spirited here to bring Dylan back to safety. That conceit, together with believing in mumbo jumbo, is testimony to just how exhausted I was. I had not noticed it at the time, but now that I was thawing out I realized that the cold had got right into my bones.

On the drive back I thought about Ollie at Dylan's age, about how he would not let me catch him either, and about how I'd attributed that to the fear he had developed of me. Now I had to consider that my diagnosis had been wrong. There may have been fear, but beyond that there was something else: there was his Saluki side.

Because Dylan is not afraid of me at all. On the contrary, and aside from his rabbit obsession, he is a typical teenager trying his luck on the question of who has the authority around here: who is Top Dog and Master of the House? So far, all of his experiments at pushing his luck had turned out all right: he had been on roads and was still alive; he had been a long time on the missing list and had turned up safe and sound; he had tested my patience as far as it stretches and not been battered to death. Luck plays a key part in the early years of a Saluki's life; and it is luck, it seems, that determines which ones survive past those turbulent teenage years.

The Mini Epic: Luck in Spades

The following morning Trezza had to go out early, and I began the day with a couple hours of work. Dylan came up to my office and started pestering me: "C'mon, buddy, it's well past time!"

I ignored him, except to comment that it was going to be a late walk today and that he was lucky to be getting any walk at all after his dismal performance the night before. As I neared completion of whatever work I'd been able to do, I went downstairs to make an espresso. He followed, as he does, waiting for the crumbs to fall off the table. Because I remained in a bad mood with him, no crumbs fell, and anyway, coffee was the very last thing he needed. I ground the beans, tapped the coffee into the espresso pot, and set it on the stove. I poured a little milk into the small metal urn that we had brought back from a holiday in Crete, a pan that is the perfect size for foaming milk, in order to convert the espresso into a macchiatto. I thought about the writing I'd just done; I gazed out the window. I looked at the coffeepot. It always takes too long to brew. It dawned on me that there was an absence. He ought to be back for a second try at the crumbs by now, for the crust of toast that he often gets. *Where was he?* I walked through the laundry room at the back of house. The door was open. Oh shit.

***

There are three little steps that lead from the open back door to the street outside, which is a narrow road with a terrace of small houses on the opposite side only. These houses have narrow front yards; Dylan was in the yard of the third house down. *"Dylan!"* I shouted. At this alarming intervention he scampered out of the yard and headed off down the street. He turned right halfway down the terrace where a curious cut-through/tunnel between houses links the narrow road to the next parallel street. I ran to the tunnel. He was nowhere to be seen. It was like losing sight of a small child in a playground; I felt the same sort of panic. He was not even wearing his collar. He has a tattoo in his ear, and he is microchipped: there are these ways of identifying him, but without the collar he has no phone numbers on him, and there is no handle by which to get hold of him either. I called his name. Nothing. I ran through the tunnel, and looked up and down the parallel street. Still no sign. The tunnel exits mid-street; it's about one hundred yards to either end, and at both ends there are two-lane one-way roads that carry a reasonable amount of traffic. Which way to go? It was a fifty-fifty call. I chose uphill. I ran, looking side to side into all the front yards. Still no sign. I hit the top. Across the two lanes is an insurance business with a grassed front, flower beds, and a parking lot that holds about thirty cars. At the far side of this there's a grassy bank. Dylan was on the grassy bank. He had crossed the two lanes of traffic and the parking lot and he was still alive. He was doing well. I didn't bother to call his name, as that was bound to inspire him to race on. I ran across the road. Even in my panic I was feeling remarkably pissed off. I'd had this once before with Ollie, but on that occasion I was a novice dog owner, one who had let him free where I shouldn't have: that was really my own fault. In this instance I knew for certain that the back door hadn't been left open, but I also knew that it has (or rather, it had) a lever handle, that it clearly hadn't been dead-bolted, and that Dylan had let himself out. Even while I was running I was working out what must have happened, getting my story straight for when I had to tell Trezza we were back to being a one-dog family because Dylan had been flattened by a truck. He is a smart boy, he had watched how it was done, had seen his chance, and had opened the door himself; it was a certainty. As I approached, still twenty yards away, he caught sight of me, jumped off the grassy bank onto the pavement and headed east toward Winterton-on-Sea. He cornered hard on the first left, a hundred yards farther along, and disappeared from view once more. It becomes immediately suburban around that corner, big houses with big yards, many new and exciting spaces to explore and in which to conceal oneself. One backyard leads onto another and eventually there is the wood where he used to run free with his cartoon ears when he was very young. Maybe he wouldn't be flattened, maybe I would just lose him completely, not knowing where he was, or whether he was dead or alive. I turned the corner into those suburbs. It's a steep hill. There was no sign of him. I ran to the first house on the left where I know they keep dogs. No, not there. I ran to the second house. Nothing. I looked across the road where a high wall protects a small development of houses. Surely he couldn't have cleared that? There's an opening in the wall, one I had never noticed before. I stood listening. I could hear nothing. I was fucked. I had really lost him. Suddenly, he walked out of this opening, the one that I had never noticed before. He stood on the pavement looking a little disoriented. "What am I doing here, Master?" he seemed to say.

***

Without the episode of the night before, I think he might have frozen when I first spotted him in the yard of the house three houses down. But the rabbit madness was still in him; it was like an acid trip and he was having a flashback. That was what was up. I crossed the road, saying, quietly but sternly, *"Dylan: Stay."* He stayed, and I crouched down, picked him up, and carried him home, the only way you *can* transport a collarless dog, short of dragging him by his tail, which is not recommended. He weighs about sixty pounds. He is not the easiest animal to carry, lengthwise, and I thought he might get into a squirm at some point, too, so I kept ahold of a little of his pelt, as a handle. A group of teenagers on the other side of the two-lane highway pointed and laughed, as if I might be the sort of simpleton who had wholly misinterpreted the idea of "taking the dog for a walk." I noted that the traffic was slowing down, to see what kind of NFN (Normal for Norfolk) type scene we had going on here. Dylan never squirmed at all. In fact, he sat regally still; he seemed to enjoy being ferried about in this way, as if it was right and proper, as if I had finally got the hang of the way in which our power relationship ought to work.

***

I had no keys on me, but on the other hand I had also left the back door wide open. That had turned out quite well, allowing the burning fumes from the exploding espresso machine to escape into the outside air. I stepped indoors, set Dylan down, once again resisting the urge to kick him on the backside, hard. I locked *and bolted* the back door, put a chair up against it, and then I went to the stove to turn the gas off. I lifted the espresso pot, which fell from my hands, splashing the final dregs of the coffee onto the floor and up the baseboards. I was left holding a Bakelite handle. This had come away in my hand, having reached the melting point of Bakelite, which must be fairly hot. I ran my scalded fingers under the cold tap for a couple of minutes and watched as the welts came up. It was okay, I didn't need a coffee anyway; this was a moment to follow my father's example on the correct way to proceed when severely testing moments present themselves. I poured a large whiskey. I could never drink the stuff in the daytime though, so I just slumped over the countertop sniffing at it and trying not to cry. And then I drank it anyway. I looked in on Dylan: I had locked him in the laundry room. He was fast asleep in his basket. It hadn't been much of a walk, but it had been a tiring adventure all the same. I went upstairs and apologized to Ollie for having him miss out on *his* walk but, I said, I better not take you out now, boy, because if anything happened I might fail the breath test and then, you know, you might be removed from my custody. He can regard you with a very far-away look sometimes; his deep brown eyes turn slightly orange and look a bit stoned, as if he has been in yurt in Mongolia smoking a pipe with his blood brothers. You are beneath his dignity. Anyway, he cares not a row of buttons whether you take him out or not, he is perfectly happy here, thinking his thoughts and being aloof. "Thank you, Master, you are dismissed," he seems to say. "I discard you."

I kissed him on the head, for not being his brother, and then I went and lay down on my office floor, which is covered in rough seagrass. It is not particularly relaxing for a lie-down, but it is more relaxing than looking after Dylan.

The Age of Anxiety

I am not a naturally apprehensive person, but I was becoming so. Soon there would be nowhere left that was safe to take this animal. I really did not want to rule the beach out of bounds, because I don't just go there for them, I do it for myself, too. I could take Ollie out on his own, of course, but that would entirely miss the point and allow the rabbits to win. I gave it the skip for a few days anyway, and instead went local; I took them to the hazardous university campus where we met up with John and Jeff and Leo and Milla, the grumpy old men and their faithful canine companions. I brought them up to date with the details of the epic. "Naughty boy, Dylan," they both said, with twinkles in their eyes that represented a secret handshake, one that meant, "Psst: actually—well-done, mate. You are not a mere callow domestic pet, you are a fierce brave hunter and a free man."

There was a new dog around, a jet-black Great Dane named Solo. We had first met Solo when he was eight weeks or so; he was about the same age as Dylan. Great Danes really are big lumps, Solo was nearly as tall as Ollie even then, and everybody comments on Ollie's height. Although Solo was about Dylan's age, he was not allowed off the leash to play all that much since Danes are a breed that require a good deal of protection for their muscles and tendons and bones in their youth. Solo's owner was a lively woman named Melody, who was not very tall. Over the course of a few months, as Solo shot up, equilibrium was more or less achieved, heightwise, between dog and owner. Solo was a handful, one of the most unruly animals around—there were moments when, beside him, Dylan could give the impression of being a rather docile and pensive creature. But Solo wasn't really a bad seed, he was simply one of those cases who seems to have a natural talent for causing, finding, and attracting trouble. Melody was a striver, one who tried everything to improve the behavior of her charge. Long leashes, short leaches, neck zappers (I never got around to buying one; they seem slightly evil to me), nothing made much difference. The problems were worse, she said, when she was out alone with him, when he took it upon himself to become overprotective of her, growling at every dog that came by, and at some humans, too. I could sympathize with this—it was a modus operandi that Ollie had been putting into development. At a certain point we were comparing notes on how it might be possible to correct the matter. Melody had gone the whole nine yards and had booked Solo to have his crown jewels removed: one suggestion that had been made to her was that it was his high testosterone level that was responsible for a large amount of the trouble, that he was giving off pheromones that were a provocation to other male dogs. Ollie's equipment was long gone, so having anything down there removed was not an option in his case. By all accounts it wasn't making much difference to Solo either, though Melanie said that it does take months to come into effect.

Ollie had been quiet for too long, I knew that. Something had to turn up, and here it was. What had begun as an exclusive contract on bashing Dylan up but stepping in to defend him should anyone else try it, or be perceived to be trying it, had begun to escalate into a more sinister variation whereby he fended off all comers. If any animal we didn't already know came into sight, he was belting up to it with his back up, baring his teeth, sometimes even snapping at it. Suddenly I was spending half my life running up to grab ahold of him and apologizing on his behalf. And as with Melody and Solo, he was even worse when it was just him and Trezza and Dylan. We kept putting him on the leash and telling him no, then letting him go again when the coast was clear. Dylan took not the smallest notice of any of this, save to take a minor body swerve out of the way of any flashpoint that appeared to have genuine potential or the threat of real action. Ollie's "attacks" actually amounted to less than they seemed—he was not sinking his teeth in, he was just issuing a warning, though you needed to have a keen eye to spot the distinction. It got to the point where we had to keep recalling him and returning him to his leash the instant any other animal came into view, and we had to be quick about it, too, because once he was off, he was off. Plenty of owners were beginning to avoid us: it was like his early days all over again. But back then he was just a slight, feather-weight lunatic who some odd, uptight onlookers seemed to think was a nasty piece of work. Maybe these objective observers recognized the potential in him, because now he actually *did* look the part.

***

One day Trezza came home with a terrible cloud over her. What happened? I asked. She did not need to say a word for me to know that something had occurred.

This was what it was: she had taken the two of them out of the car at the edge of a meadow on the far side of the university. At the same time, a man had been getting a retriever out of a four-by-four. He was a grumpy-looking man, she said, one who gave Ollie a funny look. Knowing that retrievers, along with all other breeds, were now vying to top the charts on Ollie's blacklist, she held them back to allow the man and his dog time to clear the area away to the far side of the field, where it becomes wooded with paths. They were practically out of sight, she said, by the time she let Ollie free. The moment she did so, he hared across to the retriever and attacked it. He had gone a long way out of his way to do this; the animal represented no danger to either himself or Dylan or Trezza. Ollie was actively looking for trouble. Trezza said she had run after him, shouting and issuing admonishments, which had had no effect whatsoever. When she got to the man, he was throwing sticks at Ollie and saying he'd report the dog and that it ought to be put down. He said he'd seen him before, and that we were irresponsible owners. Trezza said he was shouting and cursing. At this point I got her to describe the man, his dog, and his car to me in detail. I was looking for a way out for Ollie, hoping that we'd at least met before and that the retriever had started something or some such. But nothing in the description rang any bells: if he had seen Ollie up to his stuff before, it must have been from a distance, or maybe somebody had said to him to watch out for that wild lurcher. None of this helped, it only made it worse. It meant that Ollie was developing a reputation, a bad thing in the dog world: that sort of stuff reflects on the owners. Trezza went on to say that it had been a real effort to pull Ollie off the retriever; she had had to swing a boot at him, and even after that he'd still persisted. The only saving grace was that he had not drawn blood. "And how was he after this?" I asked.

"Bloody normal," she replied, "as if nothing had happened." Though I knew exactly how this was meant, Ollie is never entirely bloody normal, as if nothing has happened, as the following episode, which took place during this same period, will confirm.

The Incident of the Pig's Ear

After their breakfasts of dry feed and tripe, Ollie and Dylan typically take their post-prandial snacks to their respective beds while I wash dishes and make my espresso in the (new) espresso pot. One morning I became aware of a mild whimpering coming from the direction of Ollie's penthouse. *Odd,* I thought. This was followed by more whimpering, a little less mild. What the hell is he up to? Has he injured himself going upstairs? (This would be a definite possibility.) The whimpering became insistent, and suddenly escalated to urgent. I ran to his room, where I found him lying in his basket looking

179

rather desperate. He had got his pig's ear lodged in the back of his jaw; he had both bottom and top sets of teeth stuck into it, each at an awkward angle. He could not unclamp his mouth and was about to asphyxiate himself. I levered the thing free while he continued to whimper and put up an active resistance to what I was doing. "Poor Ollie," I said once I'd freed him from the hazard. I stroked his head for a while and then I offered him the ear back: he disregarded it. It would be months until he forgot this episode and felt able to face pigs' ears again. For now they were not a safe food item, they were a public danger. I turned around. Dylan has a sixth

Mad, bad, and dangerous to know: nothing too salty
or with sharp edges for me, please.

sense and a radar for happenings involving leftovers. He was hanging around the edge of the door frame with his eyes fixed on the half-eaten snack. Ollie picked it up ever so gingerly, using just his front teeth, and carefully tucked it under his duvet. Dylan went up to the edge of Ollie's basket and lay down trying to look cute. Ollie growled quietly at him. Dylan shuffled backward six inches, maintaining the cute look. He would remain there, to no avail, for another thirty minutes while Ollie regarded him unblinkingly, until he finally gave up.

The Age of
Anxiety—Continued

I did not regret bringing Dylan into the family, because by now, notwithstanding his appalling behavior as far as rabbits were concerned, his howling, and his singing (which had not abated with age, as I had imagined while driving out to the epic: that was just a false dawn and a one-off), I was very much in love with him; in a toss-up regarding who I adored more between the two of them it was absolutely even. My main misgiving about the whole project was this ripple effect in the behavior of Ollie. I could not have predicted it, but it was here, so I had to deal with it. I avoided this for as long as possible.

I was reluctant to take the obvious measure: the purchase and fitting of a muzzle. The last thing I wanted to see was my dear little boy skulking around the place looking like Hannibal Lecter. Not only would it send out all the wrong signals, but you can imagine how much he'd like it, and how many new ways he would find of engorging parts of his head and generally injuring himself on such a device, perhaps by getting it trapped in the teeth of a German shepherd he had gone over to "attack" without considering the fact that he had effectively been disarmed. Because, of course, you can easily imagine the following: fitting Ollie with a muzzle would do nothing to change his behavior. Not only can he be a bear of very small brain, but he is also a creature of fixed habit. The fixed habit he was in at the moment was of regularly shaping up to go fifteen rounds. But as we can count "unpredictabilty" as one of his key characteristics, this ought not to be the case forever; my hope was that just as the syndrome had developed, it might, with repeated tellings off, undevelop.

***

But. Here we are one Saturday morning, out with Jeff and Milla and Leo and John. Weekends are always more chancy than weekdays because this is when weekend dog walkers emerge. These are not hardcore veterans such as ourselves. I assume they have real jobs that curtail their free time and that their dogs just get a tour around the block Monday to Friday, and only see the great outdoors on Saturday and Sunday. There are plenty of fair-weather walkers, too; you often get consecutive days in the British summer where one evening is lovely and the next is a monsoon. It will be like a dog show on the nice night; it will just be us, Philip, two stray hikers, and a hobo during the monsoon. Weekend dog walkers can be irritating, because they are simply not used to the rough and tumble that the veterans' dogs dish out. They are not as irritating as cyclists and joggers, though, those Lycra-clad legions who seem to think that if *they* are there, cycling or jogging, then it goes without saying that these fields are either a cycle path or a running track and what the hell are we doing allowing *dogs to roam free* on their *private terrain*. I have perfected a look of utter disdain to which I treat them in return for the looks of out-of-breath revulsion they give me. This battle of icy stares gets thrown right out of kilter when I *myself* am jogging with my dogs somewhere behind me. This is an activity in which we can indulge ourselves on a nearby lake on the east side of Norwich, at Whitlingham, where the sequence of landscape features goes lake, path, River Yare. This arrangement limits Dylan's opportunities to go anywhere much other than backward and forward along the path. Under these circumstances the first thing the jogger sees is me, a fellow jogger (there is undergrowth between the river and the path, and it is here that the dogs are to be found, rolling in fox poop among the grasses and nettles). We joggers nod the friendly jogger-to-jogger nods. Ten strides on I look back to see where Dylan is. As he appears I see the buttocks of the fellow jogger clench and his stride change. Dylan is not bombing toward him, he is doing nothing of the sort. He is well away. He couldn't care less about joggers; he gives the merest glance of casual disinterest as he passes at a distance of five yards. "C'mon, Dylan, there's a good boy," I shout. The buttocks clench tighter. They are clenching because they have seen, and nodded to, a retrograde jogger, one who lets his *dog roam free!* I have brought shame on the name of jogging. Still, it could have been so much worse. There is Ollie, too—there is a *pair of them.* But they do not see Ollie because he is down by the riverbank. He has not been in the mood for poop-rolling; instead he is conducting a staring match with a swan. There will be a birdwatcher down there waiting to tell me off for allowing him to interfere with nature like that, but I seldom give birdwatchers the opportunity to have a word. They are another lot who are anti-dog. I have a good birdwatching friend, one who has owned a German shepherd in the past. *He* doesn't hate dogs at all, au contraire, but he has confirmed their general unpopularity among his sect. The reason for this is obvious: the birdwatcher has been staking out one of our feathered friends for three hours, trying to get a good picture or something; Ollie and Dylan come along, pile into the undergrowth, and frighten the bird away. I can see their point: it is for this reason that I jog on as if blithely unaware of anything remiss whatsoever vis-à-vis my charges.

Anyway, the traffic wardens of public spaces aside, our unruly group is causing little trouble to anyone on this particular Saturday morning at the university campus because they are confining themselves to jousting with each other. There is no bother, and there is nothing to be bothered about. The weather is mild, and Jeff and John are discussing the relative fortunes and misfortunes of our usually hopeless soccer teams. We are getting to the end of our walk, going through the rough field. The rough field has a hedge that borders the top long side. A diagonal path has been worn into the rough field, forming a shortcut from bottom-right to top-left. A man and two yellow Labradors are halfway up this path. I look around to check on Ollie's whereabouts. I can't see him because he is behind the long hedge minding his own business, until suddenly he sees these two Labs and flies through the hedge, attacking first one then the other. I run after him, I shout *no*, but he keeps it up. "You little bastard," I hear the Labrador owner say among all the commotion. Finally I get ahold of Ollie's collar, tell him off, and clip him on to the leash. I hold him short while apologizing to the owner. His dogs look like the most harmless creatures in the world, I have to concede; though there are two of them, they have made no effort to work as a pair to see Ollie off. But they have not cowered either. If I had to describe their reaction I would say they had ignored Ollie, as indeed had all the rest: neither Milla, Leo, nor Dylan had been tempted to join in. It is as if the naughty boy in class had been having his daily tantrum. The owner of the Labradors is a northerner. Although he could well be a Saturday walker (in the sense that I have never seen him before), he is wearing battered-looking countryman clothes and does not look like any sort of amateur. I put in another shift of apologizing while he carefully feels his dogs all over their necks and shoulders, looking for blood. I know he will not find any because the sad fact of the matter is that by now my eye has become expert so far as this syndrome is concerned. Ollie has menaced these dogs, but he has not applied any measure of intent. All the while the man is examining his animals and pulling at their coats he is saying things. Things like, "I know it's nice to let thee dogs roam free but if ees like that thee shouldna let eem off in a public place tha knowst: thee should get eem muzzled." Broad Yorkshire, not so far from Stoke. I felt a certain kinship with the man, he was from my sector of the north-south divide. I felt as though I was letting the side down. The only explanation I could give, one that might work at all in terms of an exoneration, was that this was a relatively new streak of behavior in Ollie (who was standing at ease by my side now, as if butter wouldn't melt) and that I was clearly going to have to do something about it. It was a lame excuse, one that I could not muster up much enthusiasm to deliver. I apologized for the final time and walked back up to our group.

"Whatever gets into him?" Jeff asks, looking at Ollie with genuine wonder.

It's not the first time they've witnessed this, but it's the worst time. Milla and Ollie will flash their teeth at each other sometimes, but they are only playing. It is not like this.

"I don't know," I say. "But something has to done."

Oh Dear, Ollie, What Have You Been Up to Now?

After I outlined the details of the incident of the two Labradors to Trezza, we agreed that the time for action had arrived. I had surfed the Internet, asked other owners for their input, and had asked the vet, too. There seemed to be no easy answers, and no quick fix for whatever it was that had got into him. But for now, at least, there was a serious short-term measure that could no longer be avoided. Reluctantly, we drove Ollie to the pet shop to see what was on offer in the way of muzzles. The fact of the matter is that if you are used to seeing your animal without a muzzle, then they will all make

191

him look menacing and ugly, even the models made of calves' leather studded with diamonds. We tried a few. It was a sight I found peculiarly depressing. I was against restricting him. One of the milestones of our difficult first year was the moment when he developed enough trust in me to come back to a call (more or less) reliably: during his fearful period this was simply a nonstarter, he was always on red alert, dead set against going back to his scary master. But, though it would have made my life a hell of a lot easier, I would *not* confine him to the leash, because he needed to run. Every time I let him free I was inviting trouble, I knew that. But eventually he did become something close to obedient, and finally our relationship cemented through the idea that he could trust me, as in turn I could trust him. I felt now as though I had failed, that our mutual deal had somehow broken down. I ought to be able to persuade him not to be aggressive. That's the way it should work. He should listen to me: even though he doesn't understand English, he understands tone of voice and body language—he should be capable of picking up signals of reassurance from his master, signals that say: Hey, boy, everything's all right, there's no call for any of this. I had been quietly telling him these things each time I returned him to the car following the incidents. I had been stroking him in a way that said, Relax, Ollie; *what's the problem?*

But now here we were, with him squirming around trying first not to be put into the Hannibal Lecter gear, and trying next to remove it by thwacking his leg around the side of his head. It was the beige plastic model that looked the least bad; it was the beige plastic model that we bought. I was so opposed to the contraption that my subconscious became involved and made me lose first one, then another, and then a third muzzle, all within six weeks. The fourth was the easiest to keep, because after six weeks we could see the beginnings of an improvement, and after six weeks I could remove it more often than not, because after six weeks it was beginning to show signs of working. And when it remained on, I was becoming used to it. More used to it, of course, than those members of the dog-walking world that we know casually and see every so often. A couple of ladies, one with a spaniel, one with a Labrador, approached. Our paths had last crossed maybe three months earlier.

"Oh my word, whatever has Ollie been up to?" one of the ladies asks, shocked to see a friendly old acquaintance in the grim-looking accessory.

"He's turned a bit snippy," I say. *Snippy* is the word

I've come up with to describe him; snippy, I feel, hits just the right charming note. Snippy conjures up a peevish old man, rather than a skinhead boot-boy.

"Well, I never," she says, looking down at Ollie in wonder as he sniffs over Henry, the Labrador, through his headgear, prancing on tiptoes, his tail unfurled behind him in the "I come in peace" position. The woman looks at me. It can't be true, surely, her look says. It's *you*, isn't it? You have become one of these Munchausen's-by-proxy people and invented a syndrome for the poor animal, haven't you? Ollie suddenly lunges at Henry's neck, growling and snarling. Our paths have crossed on a narrow stretch of dirt, we are hemmed in between a hedge on one side and trees on the other. Henry scampers one way, Dylan scampers another, the spaniel scampers a third. Two out of three of us are half knocked off our feet.

"Oh," says Henry's owner. "I see." And now that she believes me, she is on her way in double-quick time, clearing the area before anything else is allowed to happen.

Well done, Ollie. You put on an excellent exhibition of proving the point there, I tell him. Good boy, I almost say. We arrive at the football fields, where the coast becomes clear. I slip the muzzle off. Here he is happy to sledge Dylan around the back of his neck and flatten him into the ground, with a little bit of vice versa; Dylan is growing and beginning to give as good as he gets, after a fashion—ultimately, he defers to his senior. There may come a day when Dylan attempts to invert the natural order and establish his dominance. Anything's possible. But Ollie has the glint of a psycho in his eye, and perhaps Dylan can see that. Philip, who has observed the developing situation, thinks the battle for dominance will happen in any event, that nature decrees it inevitable. And Philip has his views on Ollie's new behavioral syndrome, too. He makes an assessment based on the following evidence: he notes that Ollie always picks on dogs his own size, or bigger, and that it is always an adult male he is looking for.

"He wants to test himself out, boy," Philip says. "He is *itching* for some action."

I am struck by this analysis. Although it contains the anthropomorphic note, in conflating Ollie's motivations with those found in certain types of individuals that you may encounter in playgrounds and seedy bars, I am still able to find it plausible. It is not something that has crossed my mind, because I am not often in the company of people who are looking for a fight, so I don't really understand them, whereas Philip is, and Philip does. He knows a lot of pricks, as he sometimes says. There's a patch of park around his way, and he occasionally tells me stories about the pitbull-wielding, dope-smoking, lager-drinking fraternity that hangs around there looking for trouble. He avoids it (the trouble, not the park) as much as he is able to and as part of his ongoing self-help therapy. Only once during the period that covers the writing of this book does he get into a fight himself. It takes place on the balcony of his townhouse and is provoked by a matter of such piffling triviality that he won't even tell me what it is. His feelings about the fight are mixed. He is justifiably pleased to have come out on top, because the guy was bigger than him, and at a certain point had Philip pinned to the ground while he screwed his thumb into his eye socket. Philip called indoors at this moment. "Look at this, Jayne," he told me he'd said, "he's fighting like a bleedin' girl." After making his comment, Philip, still in the prone position, unleashed a mighty left hook, which spelled Goodnight Vienna for the big fella. "I didn't know I still had a punch like that in me," he said. He was proud of the hit, and proud to have won, but he was sorry it had to start in the first place. And then he was sorry he had to deal with his friends from the local police who were on the scene like a flash since the neighbors "had been pressing their panic buttons left, right, and center like full house at the bingo, boy."

Of course, Diddley is under no threat. Though Ollie always growls at him as soon as he is in the car, for invading his personal space and getting in his way, he allows him in: he does not stand on the tailgate snipping away. He is happy to have him around. As Philip watches over Ollie, and both identifies, and identifies with, his desire to go fifteen rounds, it is his instinct to self-help therapy that gets the upper hand. Neither of us wants to see Ollie in the muzzle, and as we walk together it is taken off as soon as is safe, if it is even put on in the first place. We will be on the far side of the field, with no one around. Philip will be looking for a good stick to throw and talking about Denman, when a pair of figures appear in the middle distance, one man and his dog. "Look there, boy," Philip will say. "What is that coming along, is it one of them Airedales? Are they on the hit list, boy?" he asks, taking ahold of Ollie's collar for me, as insurance.

"They certainly might be," I say in reply, as I clip Ollie on to the leash, "what with them being biggish and brownish."

Restriction was always safer than being sorry. Pass by with the leash held short, say a cheerful "Hello" to dog and owner, even lean down to pat the dog, "Look, Ollie, he's fine, see," then let him go when the coast was clear. This was the technique I adopted most of the time, because in the early days of muzzling, Ollie continued to dive in. One afternoon I risked taking the dogs (one savage, one manic rabbiter) back up to the beach together. There was no one in sight, but they do shift like lightning up there and "no one in sight" is a status that can change in seconds. I rounded a corner of dune a few moments later than they had rounded it and came across the classic spaniel/Labrador combination. They were in the company of a nuclear family. All was quiet for a moment, as the preliminary sniffing took place, and then Ollie dived at the Lab's neck, growling and baring his teeth and, even within the confines of the muzzle, managing to look like a public menace. "Oh," said the woman, as I grabbed ahold of him and clipped him on while she edged her small daughter out of harm's way, picking her up. "Is that why he's wearing that?" (Of course, with his greyhound looks people were able to assume that he was an ex-racer who had to be muzzled simply as a precaution against bombing after small dogs and hares.)

"Yes," I said, "he's become a bit snippy lately."

"Well, good for you," the woman replied. "Because some people just let wild dogs run free, don't they, and that's not really fair to everybody else."

The small boy of the family looked at Ollie. His expression was curiously mixed, one of mild fear and awe. It's rather exciting, isn't it, to be up close to a wild animal, and equally reassuring to see that he is not in a position to stick his teeth into you. I never went in for explications stating that Ollie would not attack humans; it seemed to me that this much would be clear to all—that his only targets were others of his kind—but from a small boy's point of view it takes no leap of the imagination to envisage the mortal danger. In this moment, as if I didn't know it anyway, I was able to feel that we were doing the right thing by fitting the ghastly muzzle. Trezza almost actively liked the device: she had greater confidence in taking them out on her own now that she knew that, "he couldn't do any damage."

At the end of a beach walk, it's Ollie's habit to stage a lie-down protest against the impending "going home." If you catch him about four hundred yards from the parking lot and attach the leash you can coax him back, though he will try several sit-down protests en route. If you are daydreaming at the four-hundred-yard mark then, as you near the parking lot, you will suddenly remember about him and will turn to see that he is three hundred and fifty yards away, sitting immobile and to attention. "C'mon, Ollie," you call. "Come and get a biscuit!" You can repeat either of these expressions as many times as you like for all the difference it'll make. You can hide behind one of the boat sheds, as if you've gone. That won't shift him either. Peep around the corner, you will see that he has not moved a muscle. Walk all the way over to the beat-up station wagon, make a big show of letting Dylan into the back and feeding him treats, then conceal yourself behind the vehicle. Ollie will stay put. A couple of old ladies will pass by adjacent to him, at a distance of, say, twenty yards. They will pause and look all around. Is it a setup? Are they on *Candid Camera?* Or is it the case that the poor creature has been abandoned? Perhaps it's a setup, because he certainly looks well trained to sit still. They take a few steps forward, continuing to look all around. One stops. The other is less bothered about the dog than her friend and she moves forward, pulling the other on by the arm. The first one stops again. She is reluctant to leave it at this; they should *do something,* shouldn't they? Ollie remains totally impassive, keeping up his game of statues. If he looks at the ladies at all, it is only by moving his eyes. At this point I come forward, emerging from the distance.

"Is he with *you*?" they say.

"After a fashion," I reply.

One evening when there were no old ladies to alarm, I stayed by the car and out of his sightline while I rolled a cigarette. I was genuinely interested to see how long he could keep it up. After a while I smoked the cigarette. I gave it half an hour. I gave it thirty-five minutes. I gave it forty minutes. Once three-quarters of an hour had elapsed, I had reached my boredom threshold and I went to fetch him. He seemed completely indifferent to this turn of events, to his long-lost master showing up.

Toward the end of the beach walk during which he had sprung at the Labrador and scared the small boy, Ollie dropped to the sand for his moment.

Here is the place where he clearly wants to live. I sat beside him and tickled him behind the ears with my one free hand. He was completely relaxed, off duty. There was no one who needed seeing off or attacking. "Ollie," I said, "you are a strange creature."

In my other hand, I had Dylan's leash. Dylan was at the end of it, staring fixedly toward the parking lot.

Fetching Dylan

The Jean-Paul Sartre of lurching.

Dylan has no time for this angst and nonsense. Dylan does *not* want to live here even if there are many fine and sporting rabbits to hunt down. Dylan wants to go where it is warm and dry, to where there is a plentiful supply of biscuits, tripe, chicken, bacon, steak and lamb, numerous snacks of crusts of toast with butter, and hide chews between meals, and a selection of beds. Dylan looks down at his brother. You are such a prima donna, Ollie, he seems to be saying. To confirm Dylan's point, Ollie does not even bother to return his look, preferring to study the sand, in which, no doubt, he is finding God in every grain.

Identity Crisis

In an ideal world, I would prefer that when we went away we left the dogs in the care of friends. But you cannot, in all good conscience, expect anybody to deal with Ollie and Dylan. They are like driving a temperamental old car, the kind in which you need to depress the clutch before turning the key in the ignition (because the hand brake doesn't work so it's always left in gear), where you need to return the choke at the precise moment before it floods (otherwise it stalls), where you have to be on standby when gathering momentum because the gearshift routinely flies out of third, where you try to leave plenty of space behind you because the brake lights don't work, and which you don't take out in the rain because the windshield wipers don't work either. They are like that sort of car except they are a Ferrari and a Masserati rather than a couple of Fords. They are especially dicey because Dylan, in particular, has no brakes, while Ollie has faulty steering: he routinely over-corners when racing circuits with Dylan to the extent that he finishes up right off the track, which is typically in the next field along. Once there he saunters around pretending to be interested in the fascinating grass, as if nothing had happened that he had not intended to happen, and once there he will also go deaf. Once again, the expression, "C'mon, Ollie!" will be the one he finds particularly hard to hear. It is not just the study of botany that detains him; there is the wounded pride, too. He will return only when he thinks Dylan has forgotten, which can take some time.

No, it is a specialized business taking them out, twice daily. One I would not burden even an experienced dog-owning friend with. So: the kennels it is.

Usually I give them a good exercising early on the morning of their impending incarceration, in order to treat them to a last good blast before dropping them off at camp. The kennel is about twenty miles south, in the direction we are usually heading, to London, Stansted, or one of the Midlands airports. They have no sooner finished their breakfasts than I am calling them. "C'mon, boys, time for a second walk." In Dylan's case, okay, it's his first time kenneling, how is he to know? But for Ollie, well, he has been on the inside a few times now, but for each impending visit he comes downstairs as though it's situation normal, which he ought to know cannot be true. They are trusting creatures, who have so little control over their own destinies; I feel sorry for them in these moments, for what is about to happen to them. They say dogs have very short memories, and forget anything that happened more than five minutes ago. Not quite: they can certainly remember someone they only met once, six months earlier, providing that person gave them a biscuit, but it's true that they have no memory for this sort of thing. They must imagine they really *are* getting a bonus walk; the truth for dogs—as for certain young men when invited out for a drink—is that the great outdoors is an offer they find impossible to refuse.

They arrive at the kennel in an atmosphere of high excitement, the sounds and scents of many new dogs are heady in the air. It's like going to the amusement park (after two hours you've had enough). The kennel has changed hands. Ollie loved the previous owner, Anne, and vice versa, and I worried things would be different under the new owner, Darryl. But actually not, he seems to love her, too. Dylan is too keen to see what the hell is going on through the other side of the main gate to be showing love to anyone; he leaves us without a backward glance. Ollie on the other hand, love of Darryl or not, is always looking over his shoulder as he is led away together with the selection of security blankets that Trezza has packed for him. I feel a pang as we drive off, but I know they are safe here, and this is the important thing. I heard a story of a dog that was left by one owner with another, and that this dog escaped and was run over and killed. Imagine coming back from vacation to that; imagine being the looking-after owner waiting to break the news. You have the peace of mind that this will not happen at a kennel. When Ollie stayed there in the era of Anne, he was still a sometimes sickly animal, a legacy of his poor start in the forest, we always thought, suffering from the effects of a scavenger's diet and an absence of mother's milk. Ollie always loses a bit of weight in the kennel; he is naturally antsy and on top of this there is the stress of not living in his penthouse anymore. On one occasion when we picked him up he looked particularly skinny and none too well. Anne said he'd been eating but that there was diarrhea, too. She was concerned about him. We took him to the vet, who diagnosed *Campylobacter jejuni*, a bacterial condition. This can lie dormant in the gut causing no damage and then can be triggered by stress, the vet said.

The kennel stresses Ollie out less now, certainly not enough to make him feel poorly; additionally he has Dylan to keep him company and to make his life more interesting—they share a duplex, where I presume they spend time plotting their escape. Dylan would be the perfect inmate for a canine *Great Escape* movie. There's a large exercise pen within sight of the duplex; they are taken there several times a day for a run. I can only imagine his frustration during all those hours when it is not his turn to be in the run. While I lie on the beach I picture him working on the scheme for the tunnel that will take him there, and I picture Ollie's contribution to the Escape Committee: You take the big shovel, kid. Let me know when you see light.

This is all in my imagination, though. When we arrive to pick them up a week later, and as they tune in to our voices, I can see Ollie kangarooing in his pen, head-butting the top of the cage, which is a good height and which would not be in head-butting reach for many dogs. You will never see him more animated. He drags Darryl over to us and he leaps up and kisses our faces. You will never see him more affectionate. He has the crazed, glazed look in his eyes that you see on the faces of the innocent outside the courthouse minutes after the verdicts are given in miscarriage of justice trials. It does not last for long, his expression; Ollie is back to normal within twenty-four hours.

Dylan, on the other hand, refuses all eye contact as his release warrant is served. He launches himself un-invited into the back of the car, and he sleeps all the way home. He pauses in the kitchen only to eat, and then he sleeps again, as does his brother. And when they wake up, it is only for a second before they sleep some more. I was in Berlin during the 2008 European Soccer championships. A group of us watched the epic Turkish comeback game against the Czech Republic. Berlin has the third largest Turkish population of any city in the world: only Istanbul and Ankara have more. Minutes after the final whistle, the streets were on fire, there was a cavalcade of traffic with singing, shouting, dancing, air horns, and whistles, followed by more singing, shouting, dancing, air horns, and whistles. No one was allowed to sleep that night. I imagine the kennel after lights-out is like Berlin on a big night for the Turks; small wonder that back home it's time to catch up on rest. When not sleeping, Dylan spends two whole days going about his business without engaging with us *at all*. Many owners report that sulking takes place and that they are effectively sent to Coventry by their pets, post-kenneling. But it is not this with Dylan. He would not know how to sulk, but he does have the capacity to forget who he is. Like a genuine amnesia case, he is lost within himself. Even his motor functions are dubious: try hypnotizing him with an acorn on a string, his eyes won't flicker. Since he has been with us he has been given two general anaesthetics (for small injuries to a toe and a pad) and it is the same with these. When he comes around from the knockout he has lost all sense of himself. He sits on the sofa crying. And crying. And crying. There is nothing you can do to help. His pitch of crying is in the range that is most piercing to the human ear, and most distressing to the human soul. Twenty-four hours passed before he suddenly snapped out of it.

His identity crisis lasts longer after the kennel than

it does after the jab. It is forty-eight hours before he comes to himself. You turn around to see how he is getting on. He is leaning off the sofa eating your sock. He catches your eye. "Ha!" he says, "wondered how long it'd be before you noticed I was here." He slips off the sofa to nuzzle at your pocket: Got any biscuits in there, buddy?

Thank God, the real Dylan is back.

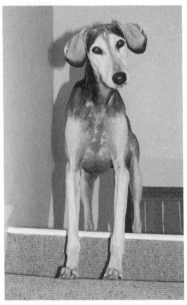

I am not a number, I am a free dog.

Extracurricular Activity

During the worst of Ollie's aggressive behavior, we were invited to a lure coursing event at the East of England Showground, arranged by an online lurcher rescue website called Lurcher Link. We had heard of the activity, but we did not really know what lure coursing involved, and although Dylan comes from a lineage that excels both in the field and in the show ring, it was not our intention to "work" him in either of these ways. I sent Karen, the breeder, a picture of him at about eight months, which she much admired.

"He'll show," she said, meaning he could aim to go to an exhibition show.

"Is there money in that?" I asked.

"No," she replied. "It'll cost you."

That finished that matter for me, and finished it in a happy way. I feel I have already gone far enough down the road of the Cult of the Dog Owner without additionally devoting hours of my life to driving all over the continent in order that some dubious individual can cast an opinion regarding whether Dylan is Best in Show or not. I can't say that the thought of showing hadn't crossed my mind even before this brief conversation with Karen: beauty being in the eye of the beholder, I think, like every other member of the Cult, that our boys are the best. I don't need anyone to tell me *that*.

***

This lure coursing was another matter, because it was clearly sport, and sport is somewhat different from a beauty pageant. We arrived at the showground to find that we had a celebrity in our midst. People would pass by, or approach directly, pause, do a double-take, and say, "Excuse me, but is that Ollie?" He receives a little of this around Norwich, too, and I think people are some-times slightly disappointed that he looks so normal. But then they offer a hand that reveals a treat, from which he backs away suspiciously. Ah! they are then able to say, either out loud, or just in a look that crosses their face: Ah!—that's more like the Ollie from the book! At the showground, Ollie got used to the fuss: after half an hour of it he was practically signing autographs. All the while I was tickling him behind the ears, quietly murmuring, "Good boy, Ols" to keep him sweet, while I remained on silent red alert regarding the aggression thing. *That* might not sit all that well with his superstar status, or on the other hand perhaps it would do no harm: a tantrum or two is only to be expected from a drama queen such as himself. Fortunately, here was the thing: by and large, fellow hounds were excluded from the hit list. But even if we had arrived in the middle of a hundred or more assorted Belgian shepherds, boxers, and black Labradors, I think Ollie would have had the sense not to have taken them on single-handed. Dylan, who had never joined in with his shenanigans in any event, could hardly be relied on as backup in circum-stances such as these (or in any other circumstances). Seeing himself so vastly outnumbered, Ollie instead put on an Oscar-winning charade of being a Special Peace Envoy.

Meanwhile, Dylan's sights were elsewhere. This "chasing after things" business could not have been any further up his alley and was something that he clearly fancied his chances at. I could tell this by the way he was straining at the end of his leash, and bouncing on his back legs with his tail in the air. Lure coursing involves setting dogs off in singles or in pairs after a bundle of plastic bags that are attached to the end of a wire. The wire recoils at a rapid speed in a zigzag across a large field. At the sharp points of the zigzag there are a couple of traffic cones: extra marks or merits are given if the animal goes between the cones as it corners, rather than flying into or beyond them. Quite a lot of the animals there were experienced at it. We, on the other hand, hadn't even got an entry, and Dylan was technically disqualified because he was purebred and not a lurcher. However, a dispensation was made that allowed them to have a fun run. Ollie went first; he chased the plastic bags three yards and then stopped. "Good boy," I said to him. "You were not so foolish as to be taken in by that, were you?" He gave me a look that said, Beneath my dignity, to be honest. Dylan went next. He flew up the field as if born to it (which of course he was) and returned some minutes later wearing an expression like the one you see on the faces of young children when they get off their first-ever ride on a roller coaster.

Dylan was only allowed the one go-through, however many times he asked for more, so we walked him around and let him off for a run away from where the coursing took place. We stayed awhile, pausing frequently to talk the dog-talk with fellow owners, and in so doing Ollie met, and was in close proximity to, many more—and new—hounds than was typical of an average day, some of which were big and male, one or two with perhaps a little element of "C'mon then" about them. There was not a bit of trouble, and this, I think, was where he reached the top of his curve and began to slide down the other side of the graph. It may have been accidental, it may have simply chimed with the moment and it was going to happen anyway, but it seemed to me that being in this crowd of his own kind signaled a change in Ollie's attitude.

Who's That Lady?

O ur house is an end unit. Those adjacent properties with the small front yards—one of which Dylan was investigating prior to getting his mini-epic under way—are situated in a narrow road that runs at a right angle to our place. Because the road is narrow with a perplexing array of signs at each end (what does the one where the motorbike jumps over the car actually mean? Is it a one-way street, or what?), it is also quiet. One evening the peace was gently disturbed by one of our neighbors, Adrian, who lives directly opposite our driveway. He is a lovely neighbor because, as I remember it, he disturbs the peace quite often by rehearsing songs from musicals. He's a professional musician, a pianist, who accompanies vocalists who come to his front parlor to rehearse for forthcoming productions at the local theater. I am essentially opposed to the stage musical, but when I hear these songs out of context, drifting up through the window of my attic office in the middle of a Tuesday afternoon, I am more than happy to hear them. But it was not "The hills are alive with the sound of music" with which Adrian was breaking the air on this quiet evening; rather, he was doing so by calling out a name: *Lady*. I went to my window and saw him looking up and down the street between calls. I knew immediately what must have happened. A few months earlier he and his partner had lost their cat, Peggy, who was elderly and seldom seen. Lady must be the new Peggy. Dylan, who is considerably more nosy than I am, was already standing at Trezza's office window, one floor below my attic room. The window is a sliding sash that Trezza routinely leaves six inches open at the bottom. Dylan often has his nose stuck out of that six-inch gap, conducting surveillance, sniffing at all the fascinating smells that waft by, and occasionally startling the shit out of cyclists by barking at them suddenly for no reason other than that he can (that's my boy). Lady did not respond to Adrian's calls (possibly a bit of Saluki in her?) so he went around the back to try his luck there. Soon enough the whole of our neighborhood was made aware that there had been a sighting, and they knew about it four miles away on the far side of the city, too: the racket Dylan made at cyclists was pianissimo in comparison to the volley he let fly on first spotting a black-and-white kitten padding up the pavement minding her own business. A platoon of rabbits marching up the street flipping him the bird could not have outraged him more. He added yodeling and yelling to his vocal repertoire while at the same time doing loops around the room, hurdling the battered armchair in which he naps (Trezza had picked it up secondhand for herself; it was immediately co-opted), and flying low over Ollie's head as he long-jumped Ollie's basket to complete the circuits. Ollie—wearing the wan expression of the exceptionally long-suffering—ducked slightly. Dylan stopped to attention in front of me before darting to the window, where he kept looking back over his shoulder, urging me to come and see: Look! Just *look*! Not only is that animal on the loose, it's alive, too! Where's the fairness in that?

We have had to be (more) careful with Dylan since

Lady's arrival. A couple of times on his way out for his walk, having caught a glimpse of whisker, he has dragged Trezza out the back door, down the steps, and straight into the road like a cartoon dog running away with a string of sausages. Lady, being a cat, has taken no time to work out that he will never get at her because he is always under some sort of restraint, and so, in the face of his preposterous din, she is happy to sit on a wall being a superior species. Sometimes, for a change of pace, she perches, like a partridge, on a branch of the pear tree next door, being a superior species. To Dylan, she is a squirrel with multiple attitude problems.

I was able to achieve mild retribution on Lady on his behalf just once, and this was accidental. One evening I saw her digging a hole in the front yard of a house on the main road. "Hello, Lady," I said as I passed. She turned from her digging, looked at me, and froze. I had completely spooked her: how the hell did I know her name? As a response to my low cunning and counter-intelligence, she bolted for home, where she found her front door locked and Dylan leaning out of Trezza's window belting out the old Chairmen of the Board song, "Give me just a little more time, And our love will surely grow." In order to restore order to our peaceful neighborhood, I went upstairs and attempted to distract and placate him. It took a bone *and* a pig's ear to achieve that.

Where does Ollie fit into all this unseemliness? Being aloof and feline himself, he doesn't mind cats; he plays them at their own game by ignoring them entirely. But he minds Dylan's noise pollution and his associated eccentric *antics*. If Ollie is anti anything in his still, indoor life, it is surely antics; if there is to be any eccentric behavior, it is to be done by him, not by some Lord Snooty upperclass incomer inbred like Dylan. When the younger animal has worn himself out and is happily asleep with his head resting over the side of Trezza's armchair, now is the time for Ollie to act. He walks over and, as a way of starting a lengthy bout of wrestling, takes the resting head in his mouth and mildly savages it. Dylan has neither the energy nor the appetite for wrestling, but in these circumstances he is not given a choice: once a fight has been started, it has been started. The big brother in me silently applauds Ollie's technique—the moment to mount a campaign against a younger sibling is when they are off guard, eating a bowl of cereal in front of the television. They *have* to be put in their place, and timing is the key: as they sit watching *Tom and Jerry*, laboring under the misconception that they are safe, that is the moment to shoot a rubber band at the back of their head. It is Trezza, who is the youngest in her family, and who therefore knows precisely what it's like to be on the receiving end, who eventually tells Ollie to cut it out. She flicks him behind the ear to jerk him back into his basket. He gives her the look: What!? *I wasn't even doing anything.* (That's my boy, too.)

Old Stokie Comes to Town

Old Stokie is my favorite old individual from Stoke-on-Trent, the type for whom the word *picaresque* was invented. OS is a man of many schemes and scrapes, for instance the one in which he sells "original artists' ceramics" to Americans on eBay. Fellow Stoke City soccer fan and would-be novelist—"Just look over this manuscript for me: I'll cut you in for 20 percent if it's any good"—OS unexpectedly invites himself over to Norwich. The call goes as follows:

"Winger" (he always calls me after the fictional narrator from my first novel), "I'd like to book in for Friday."

"Fine," I reply. "ETA?"

"Half past four."

"Any special dietary requirements?"

"No bloody snails," he says, "and no bloody streaky bacon wrapped around prunes with a toothpick." (He is also the type of individual for whom the word *irascible* was invented.)

The sanction on *l'escargot* and *anges en cheval* (or something) refers back to incidents that took place in restaurants in the south of France and Berlin, incidents in which I encouraged him to "try new things," incidents that resulted in him spitting out food and making his face like a toddler given an olive. It was Old Stokie who had arranged the outings: he is an expert web surfer, one of the battalion of irritating retirees who gets under your feet in airports because they have found flights to Budapest for three dollars, and an accompanying hotel deal for five bucks a night. He is always sourcing bargains, buying tickets in batches, and arranging weekend excursions away with the boys. Here is the typical OS email:

Winger: dunner forget, it's East Midlands airport at 6 am on Saturday DO NOT be bloody late like last time. PULIS OUT!

Old Stokie Comes to Town

One of the ties that binds us is that we both revile the manager of our team, not least for his unutterable dullness. There is nothing dull about Old Stokie. An ex-miner and long-haul truck driver, he has been a widower since 2001 when his beloved wife, Ann, passed away. I met him not long after this. Though he is not short of a twinkle and some suggestive patter for the ladies, there will never be a replacement for Ann; keeping busy is the way OS copes with his loss. His son, Tony (Swiss Tony, as he is known, because he is neutral in all arguments), made it his business to move in just up the road from his old man following their bereavement, in order to be near enough to look out for him. His daughter lives a couple of streets away, too. He has five grandkids whom he calls "a pain in the arse," but he spoils them rotten and worships the ground they walk on. They are about as tight a family as you could ever meet. Occasionally in conversation the subject turns to dogs: though there are none now, there has usually been one in the OS clan, all waifs and strays, and he dedicates a section of his (ahem) website to their memories. This is his entry for Judy.

Judy was my first dog and was our companion during those early years at home in The Meir. She was a terrier and had no problem whatsoever looking after herself. Dad kept pigeons and Judy kept the cats away. The sight of this little monkey tearing down the backyard was a sight to behold. In those days, bitches roamed the street at will. The consequences of that was that Judy had about ten litters of pups! Perhaps that's where I found my love of dogs because there was rarely a time when we didn't have the little buggers under our feet. The smell of a baby puppy is beautiful, too. Judy's been dead for 40 years.

Inviting himself over to Norfolk out of the blue was uncharacteristic; he had never been to see us before, and so had met neither Ollie nor Dylan, though he had heard plenty about them and seen pictures on email.

"What's the purpose of this visit, then," Trezza asked, as she crossed snails off the shopping list.

"To see the place before he croaks?" I replied.

My belief is that he is always contemplating his impending date with mortality, though his timing is not that great: about four years ago he simultaneously emailed me and another middle-class refugee from Stoke-on-Trent, Elt, asking if we would each like to give a reading at his funeral. Elt mailed me straight back: What the hell is he on about? Is he dying?

I don't think so, I said, just planning ahead.

***

He arrived on a Friday afternoon, spun his twinkle and patter and charm routine on Trezza (it worked, of course), met Dylan, who, naturally, came out to meet him, and then lit up one of the many thousands of cigarettes he smokes every day. When he went upstairs he stood at the threshold of Ollie's room and left it at that. "He'll come out and see me when he's ready," he said. Ollie had remained motionless in his basket, simply regarding OS with the look of mild suspicion that he keeps on standby for the arrival of strangers.

I made some proper food for dinner, a homemade steak and kidney pie, which I served with frozen French fries. I was roundly criticized for this: "I haven't come all this way for bloody frozen fries, Winger." I neglected to counter-mention that on the one night I'd stopped over at his place I'd been served something that came out of a box from the supermarket's house label. On Saturday morning we all went up to the beach. There was a headwind on the walk out, which caused a certain amount of weariness on the return leg. "Oi," I suddenly heard this voice calling out. "Wait a minute: you walk too bloody fast." I turned to be confronted with this tableau:

Old Stokie will sit down anywhere for a cigarette, or just for a pause, and he may turn his conversation to any subject while he's at it; he's like a permanent live staging of *Waiting for Godot*. You can't knock that. The curious point to note here is that Ollie and Dylan have pulled up with him. It must be the case that they instinctively recognize a natural-born dog lover when they meet one, and beyond that it's not out of the question that they are making some sort of allowance on account of his age, too. They read people well, I think.

From this comfortable seat, Old Stokie calls Swiss Tony on his cell phone. It is a rather nice, rather meaningless conversation. You could drop it in anywhere into Beckett's great script.

"Hello? Tone? Yes. I'm in the dunes with Winger and Trezza and Ollie and Dylan. What? No, quite nice, only a bit windy. What? Yes, tea and toast. What? Marmalade. What? Nothing, just having a smoke and talking to you."

After a while of this, and finally:

Vladimir asks his friend: Alors? On y va?

And Estragon answers: Allons-y.

In the denouement of the play, and as the final curtain falls, we see that neither of the protagonists moves on. Here at Winterton it was different. In real terms I had plenty of work to be getting on with this weekend, but, as OS dragged his carcass up off the ground, I was able, once more, to consider and appreciate the point of him. He brings a similar joy into the world that the dogs provide: while they might all three appear to be holding you up and stopping you from progressing, the fact of the matter is that they are the material that gets into my soul, without which there would be little to say and no progress to be made.

On Sunday morning I arranged to meet Philip and Diddley. We walked around the broad at Whitlingham. Philip and OS got on well, as I knew they would. I had already given Philip the buildup as Norwich's greatest tough guy; to Philip I had simply said, "Old friend coming over from Stoke, meet you down at the lake."

It didn't take long for Philip to establish that OS was an ex-miner. This was a detail that inspired him to pull up and shake OS by the hand. "Got a lot of respect for you, boy," he said. "That's proper work."

It was no later than 9 a.m., the weather was cold, the wind blowing into our faces, and we had barely gone two hundred yards, but it was soon enough for Philip and OS to begin offering each other cigarettes and sparking up. By the time they were on their second smoke of the walk, seven minutes later, they were already discussing a shared opinion. "Yes," said Philip, "he do walk too fast, boy." Before they could really develop a rap on this matter, a heron took off from the field and flew overhead. It's a beautiful sight, one that will stop anyone in his tracks, anyone except Dylan that is. Dylan lives in a wonderland of permanent hope, a world in which birds on the wing can be caught. The first time he came down here a pair of swans took flight, following the long straight ash path that parts the lake from the River Yare as if it were a runway. In one of the earliest and most memorable "blow his lungs up" moments, Dylan, who was perhaps four months then, chased them down the path until both he and they were out of sight. Bird-chasing is a habit he has yet to outgrow. Diddley and Ollie stand and watch, Ollie no doubt noting his brother's extreme stupidity, Diddley no doubt delighted to see him wearing himself out before they have their next race.

"Proper dogs," said Old Stokie as he watched this.

"That's right, boy," said Philip.

On the drive back, as we were on our way to pick up three espressos and a slice of cake for Jayne, I turned to discussing a particularly thorny issue in OS's novel, namely his overuse of the word *guy*. This guy does this, he's a great guy, he really liked this guy, he really didn't like another guy, and so on and so on. I had already mentioned this to OS the previous evening, and he had taken my editorial advice badly, saying that there was nothing wrong with the word, that I was too persnickety, and that it was bloody well staying like it was.

"What do you think about it?" I asked Philip, over my shoulder.

"That's a funny word to me," Philip said. "It's a bit American, boy."

Old Stokie was outraged—I say guy all the time, it's not American, everyone says it, and so on.

A couple of days later I received a text from Philip (advising a nap on a horse) that included, as its payoff line: "Say hello to that guy from Stoke 4 me." Philip spends a lot of time disparaging himself: just a hard-luck story from the wrong side of the tracks and whatnot. I try to discourage these ideas, keeping texts like this one to show back to him later, as proof that he is a sharp enough tool to make a nice, written joke. Where will that get me though, boy? he says. Into this bloody book about Dylan at least, I tell him.

"Write what you like," he says. "I don't mind. But make it the truth."

"Okay," I say. "That's what I'm doing anyway."

"That's all right, then, boy," he says. "Nothing wrong with the truth. Am I the hero then?"

"Yes," I reply.

A day or two later, OS texts in reply to Philip's "Say hello" text, saying to say "Hello" back and mentioning also to "wish him good luck with that horse, boy." Philip and Old Stokie have not seen the last of each other. They will meet again, next season, when, as it turns out, much-reviled manager Pulis actually achieves that promotion to the EPL.

***

We travel over to see a key match, and afterward we stay over at Old Stokie's. I wake on Sunday morning in his spare room. They are both already up and about and the first thing I hear is the pair of them complaining about how I can't make a proper cup of tea, while they simultaneously congratulate each other on their own great talent at this key life skill. I seem to be rather redundant in their lives, I think, as I rub my sore, hung-over head. Still, at least I have managed to bring them together so that that they can walk slowly, smoke cigarettes, and make world-class tea to their hearts' content.

Soon after Old Stokie and Philip's initial introduction it was judgment day for Philip. But first . . .

The Fight

Philip's prediction of the inevitable battle for dominance turned out to be a good call, though the venue took me by surprise, and kept it brief, too. I had just gone over the most dubious junction on the way up to Winterton-on-Sea. You really do have to be careful here because it is a dog-legged crossroads, and aside from any number of tractors and other heavy farm machinery being pulled about by individuals who actively enjoy holding the traffic up, there are dithering tourists to be taken into account; there is the odd boy-racer in a Subaru; there are a number of Evel Knievels on Harleys;

and then there are the time-served locals: Norfolk is overrepresented as far as ninety-year-olds, of both sexes, with two tufts of white hair, who cannot see over the top of the steering wheel even when sitting on a cushion. We had just safely navigated this junction when I was taken aback as an almighty growling and snarling racket erupted—with absolutely no fanfare, no emcee shouting, LaydeeesandGentlemennn, in fact with no prior warning at all, not even a few preliminary barks. Having dispatched one crappy old station wagon, we were driving in a new (to us) crappy old station wagon at this moment, one in which the guard net, having been dipped into a vat of "dogs hate the taste of it," was still intact. As neither of them were given to breaching this barrier, they confined their altercation to the rear area of the car. The back end was flying from side to side as they pinned each other to the ropes. More than aware that I was making my own contribution to Norfolk's road life now, I went so far as to take my eye off the road as I shouted over my shoulder at them to *stop it!*—a request that fell on deaf ears. I swerved to the side of the road and ran around the back. By the time I had lifted the tailgate they had ceased. They each turned to look at me wearing identical "It wasn't me, I wasn't even there" expressions. I poked both of them in the muzzle and told them I wanted to see no more of *that*. Who won the fight I will never know, except that it was surely Ollie, since their power relationship has changed not one bit. Perhaps it was just the traditional pre-bout trash-talking match at the press conference. Maybe the real thing is yet to come. I don't know.

That the real thing was upon us at the racetrack was in no doubt. The papers were full of it; Philip was texting me about five times a day, as well as leaving messages on my voicemail advising me to "Get stuck in, any spare money what you got: stick it on—it's a certainty, boy."

Denman Goes for Gold

Philip had sent us a Christmas card, or to be precise he had hand-delivered it in person on Christmas Day, inviting himself in for a bottle of champagne or two. The card was homemade, featuring a picture of Denman, cut out of the *Sun*, on the front, and a betting slip tucked inside. The slip was for a five-dollar double on Denman winning both the Hennessey (another big race) and the Gold Cup. The odds on the double were twenty to one, and the Hennessey was already won. That was a guaranteed hundred-dollar return, unless Denman should lose the Gold Cup (impossible and out of the question), in which case it was worthless apart from the artwork Philip had added to the ticket—a portrait of the horse's head. Philip had slips of this type littered throughout his home, small doubles and trebles and forecasts, as well as many, many single bets. Whenever he had a winner he reinvested half of the winnings in Denman. It was a simple system, one that was bound to pay off, big-time. It would be like a royal wedding when he got over to William Hill after the foregone conclusion of the finish—his confetti of investments thrown over the counter would take days to sort out, and the street party to follow would last longer than that.

As well as himself and Jayne, Philip brought another present around on Christmas Day, a present for Dylan: Diddley. That we lost only one champagne glass to gravity's pull was a minor miracle as the two of them celebrated the day in the traditional way, Diddley stealing Dylan's toys, Dylan retaliating by repeatedly humping him from behind, with time-outs given for races up and down the hall. Ollie, who is named after one Dickensian character, was now behaving like another as he sat Scrooge-like, saying "Bah, humbug" and keeping himself to himself in his penthouse upstairs. Unlike the younger animals, Ollie declined the offer of a mince pie (though he wouldn't say no to a slice of turkey).

***

At a certain point in the New Year, some time in early February, after Denman had won his final race before Cheltenham, his eighth straight win, and by twenty lengths, too, I decided that the time had come for me to take a view. I took the view that Philip was right. "Well done, boy," Philip said, shaking me by the hand for finally having the wit to think straight. I got slightly carried away by Philip's enthusiasm, and by the time the race went off I had invested more in Denman than I had ever invested in a horse before.

I go to Cheltenham each year with my friend Ben. It's a tradition for us to be there for the final two days of the four-day "Festival," as it's known. We buy our tickets well in advance, almost a year before, because we like to get seats in the grandstand, and you have to be an early bird to do that. At the beginning, the first time we went, we started out standing in the enclosures. This is all well and good provided you have gone there to spend the day drinking. If you want to see any racing, it is not the best vantage point, it is a zoo. Those colorful objects looming into the lenses of your binoculars are not jockeys on horses, rather they are hats, and the backs of other people's heads. Still, even in the knowledge of that situation, a thought insinuated itself into my mind, which was this: since I was to be driving down to where the greatest race of all time was about to take place, it would be churlish of me not to offer Philip a ride, even if the best he could hope for was to be crammed in with the sardines in the Tattersalls stable. But really I could not take Philip down, because for Ben and I there are a great many traditions in this pilgrimage, one of which is a certain choreography of chatter during the early-morning drive—ludicrous conversations about Spain and cheese and our favorite desserts and soccer players and the Pope—conversations into which I could not, in all seriousness, introduce Philip with his nonstop Denman this, Denman that, and Denman the other interjections. Also, Philip did not have a ticket for the Tattersalls, if there were even any left, and I knew he could not give up the hundred bucks or so that they would be wanting for the main enclosures, even if there were any of them left either. Because I am hopeless at keeping to the rules that I make (which is why I never entirely give

Denman Goes for Gold

up smoking, and why Dylan now frequently sleeps on our bed) I decided that Philip could come down with us and shatter our peace anyway, and that he could also get in, because I bought him a ticket online, last minute. The one thing I could not sort out for him was accommodation. The hotels around Cheltenham are fully booked up by all those who have stayed there the year before, it's a sort of catch-22: to stay there, you have to already have stayed there. Ben and I stop in Stratford, twenty miles away. This was as near to the track as we could manage the first time we did it, and we re-book, like everybody else: our hotel is an Emerald Isle occupied by the same Irishmen on each renewal. These are full of tips, opinion, and superstition—there is not one of them who does not "take a view." Each year we look out for our favorite—the fat one who wears his lucky wristwatch on his ankle, which, as he told us, makes it extra lucky, and being as it is upside down, it also tells the time in Australia.

On the opening day of the Festival, still in Norwich, I briefly met up with Philip. He and his buddies had selected the pub to see them through the four-day marathon. This—a lucky-Irishman-upside-down-Australian-time-telling-watch good omen, and a sign, for sure—was called the Quebec. I mentioned this to Philip, and he counter-mentioned to me that only grannies say stuff like that. The Quebec is ideally located across the road from a bookie. We stood outside the pub after the first day's big race, which I had popped in to watch. I mentioned I'd got this spare ticket that he could have. He was pulling heavily on a cigarette.

"But what would I owe you?"

I had thought this through. "Nothing. Take it out of the Denman winnings," I replied.

"Thanks, boy," he said.

"But you'll have to sort your own accommodation," I said. "It's wall-to-wall No Vacancies down there: perhaps you could shack up in a stable or some such?"

"I done worse, boy," he said. "I could stay up all night in a bar, couldn't I?"

"That would be one way of going about it," I replied.

***

We took the dogs out the following morning, the morning before Ben and I left. Philip ummed and aahed about whether to come down with us and sleep rough in a field, or whether to chance it and see if he couldn't get a ride down on the day—"Some bugger must be going"—and then simply ride home in our car, waving to the crowds and condescendingly chucking fivers out the windows, behavior that would befit a man of his enormous new-found wealth. At a certain point during our walk Dylan got into a tremendous sprint, with Ollie in very close attendance. "Which is which, Philip?" I asked. "Dylan is Denman," he replied, the only response he could give, since Dylan had won it by a neck. The right answer for Philip, insofar as the first and second places were concerned, was the incorrect answer for the general public. On the day of the race both the people and the pundits went all in with Kauto Star, as did principal stable jockey Ruby Walsh, who, having selected the reigning champ as his ride, ahead of Denman, had only ensured that the money continued to pile on his horse. On the track the gamblers were decked out in rosettes and floppy Cat in the Hat hats in Kauto's running colors; on the morning news it was a unanimous call: the Star would triumph, experience would win out.

Philip decided against the perils of the all-night bar or the hayloft, preferring instead to put a general SOS out for a ride on the day, but he never made it down to Cheltenham. He was particularly dismayed about this when he later heard that a man had been into his local OTB seeking him out to offer him a ride. He wasn't there at the time, and apparently, as he was led to believe, people were sent out to look for him, a story to which he gave scant credibility. As he put it: "How hard am I to find, boy? I'm only going to be in one of three places."

The Gold Cup is just over three miles—two circuits and twenty-two fences—with an uphill finish to the final straight to sort out the men from the boys. Denman tracked the leader, Neptune Collonges, for the first circuit and went to the front as he passed the packed stands after the first full circuit. Kauto was third and did not appear to be traveling all that well. There was a hush in the air. The gossip going around before the race was that 90 percent of the money was on the big two, and that that money was riding eighty-to-twenty in favor of Kauto Star, even though the ground had gone slightly soft, which was supposed to be a positive for Denman and a slight negative for Kauto. You get these lemming-like rushes of madness on race tracks, though. I have been part of one myself, at this very venue, having been one of the unhinged individuals who pushed the hopeless-at-Cheltenham-but-brilliant-in-Ireland Beef or

Salmon into short-priced favoritism for this same race a couple of years earlier (he "played no part in the finish"). The hush was the sound of the silent apprehension of the majority as they faced the prospect of being brought back to their senses with a bump. Denman was clear out in front now, taking his fences like a stag. It was magnificent jumping, there was no question he was going to tip up; the only way he was going to lose was if Ruby Walsh could kick in the turbo on the Star. As they came around the bottom corner a few furlongs from home, where, in all honesty, I still expected the worst to begin unfolding, it became clear that Ruby was struggling. Denman was eight, nine, ten lengths clear. The blood began to fizz in my veins. The greatest race of all time had become a one-horse demolition act. It was as if the uphill finish was not even there; the result was never in doubt. Jockey Sam Thomas rolled Denman home with gas to spare. He destroyed the field.

Philip and his "view" had not only prevailed, they had saved my Festival, too. I was in the middle of one of the longest losing streaks of all time; before this race I'd backed twelve non-winners in a row, but in this moment these insubstantial, piddling losses had been wiped out in a flash of pure gambling genius.

Fetching Dylan

In a crowd of race-goers it can sometimes seem as if everybody has a cell phone clamped to his ear at all times, sniffing out signals, arguing with his mistress, making bets, booking restaurants, talking to counselors and therapists. The satellites overhead become over-loaded and it's frequently difficult to get either a signal or a connection. Nonetheless, even as Denman was being led back to the winner's enclosure to accept his acclaim, I managed to contact Philip. I could not understand a word he was saying, but I was getting the impression that he was in a pretty good mood, boy.

***

The following Sunday, more than a week later, we walked the dogs around the lake. It was a vile, rainy day and there were no joggers or cyclists to make faces or to mut-ter. Joggers and cyclists are in short supply on vile, rainy days—it is one of the reasons I like them. Philip was in excellent good humor, having collected a few thousand bucks, paid a few people off, bought a few other people drinks, looked after his mother, and all the rest of it. I have no doubt that it will not be too long before he is broke again, but that is his life; the battle between himself and the bookies is the struggle that keeps him going. These moments, he tells me, of winning big are the only times he ever feels truly content. Following the walk we drive back to our place, crack open the Denman champagne that has been purchased with the Denman money. As we raise our glasses it occurs to me to ask Philip how he comported himself in the Quebec as the race unfurled.

"You got it on video, boy?" he asks.

"Indeed," I reply.

"Put it on and I'll run you through it then."

He describes the scene and stands roughly where he was, center stage in the bar, looking slightly upward to the raised screen.

"You were right near the television, then?" I ask.

"It was my big moment, wasn't it? I had to front up and brave it out."

On the first circuit he is relatively sanguine, just a few low *Gooarnns,* and *Goooarrn there boy, my sons.* As the last half mile unfolds, he is doing the occasional, unconscious, automatic, mimed giddyap. Slightly prematurely, in my view, he is celebrating: "It's all over—get the drinks in barman, on me." And as the finishing post looms ever closer he comes across slightly minimalist: he is simply nodding. It has all turned out as he knew it would, as he has dreamed it many times. He has told me about those dreams.

"What would you have done if it had gone wrong, Philip?"

"Walked out without saying a word, boy. What else could I do? But I would still have woken up the following day, wouldn't I? Life would go on."

Philip's actions inspired Dylan and Diddley into a circuit or two of our living room, including hurdling the distressed coffee table and the sofas. We whip the glasses up out of their way, and no one comes to any harm, but that is not always the case with animals. Months before the big race, the co-owner of Denman had said in an interview that he was not getting too excited about the Cheltenham bid quite yet. Just getting to the Festival in one piece would be an achievement, he said, because "being in the farming industry, and looking after animals all the time, I know there's so much that can go wrong." In the aftermath of big races the most commonly heard line, expressed by trainers, owners, and connections—win or lose—is that the main thing is that all the animals are "all back safe and sound and in one piece." Occasionally horses are lost, and they all say the same thing about that, too: that there is nothing worse than driving home with an empty box.

Sick Notes

So, the best incidental consequence of the Gold Cup was that Kauto and Denman came out of the race stripping fit, and if it remains that way there is the prospect of a renewal some time, some place in the future. But all running animals get a knock once in a while, it goes with the territory. It particularly goes with the territory if you are a lurcher/Saluki/greyhound type. You cannot fly about over all terrain at thirty miles per hour, putting who knows how much g-force through your bones and joints, without picking up something in the way of injury. Dylan had a good run for his money before he had his first serious skirmish with the medics. He'd picked up nicks and scratches in plentiful numbers (one breeder had told me that they can go into shows with these scars, that the judges deduct no marks for them as they are expected of the breed), but he had yet to receive an injury that troubled him. In this sense, as in many others, Dylan was the anti-Ollie: in his first couple of years Ollie had a season ticket to the vet. At one point he simply could not leave the house without cutting a pad: if there was no broken glass within the undergrowth, he made do with nature—on one occasion he gashed the flesh just above his ankle on the rough branch of a shrub. It required six stitches, and as Gerhard, our vet, said (and not for the first time), Ollie had been lucky: he had only just missed rupturing the tendon.

For a while we had been noticing that Dylan kept pulling up, holding his front leg lame. We carried out our own examination, and finding nothing visible, diagnosed "pulled muscle." But it went on for a while longer and did not improve, so reluctantly, we took him to Gerhard. Where Ollie was a very good patient, Dylan is not; where Ollie would stand quite still and passive, Dylan will squirm, complain, and try to escape. Still, at the outset he was not all that bad. Gerhard made a thorough examination of his leg, foot, and toes and could find nothing. "Perhaps he has something lodged in a pad," he said. "They get that sometimes, like a shard of metal, a nail, or even a splinter of wood. It goes right through and only starts throbbing after exercise. Is he worse on hard surfaces?"

"Yes," I said, "I think he is."

Gerhard went across his pads, having a good look to see if he could locate any pinprick entry points, gently applying pressure to each one in turn. He could find nothing and was beginning to scratch his head. He went back across the pads again and this time he discovered the precise coordinate of the trouble because this time Dylan jumped and yelped at full volume, directly into Gerhard's ear. You could hardly perfect a better technique for shattering an eardrum. While I was apologizing about this, Dylan, considering himself under attack, moved to bite Gerhard's arm. "Whoa there, Dylan," Gerhard said with an uneasy smile, "steady boy." A veterinary nurse came in to help. Dylan was muzzled, a device that he resisted like crazy, making it all but impossible for even three of us to hold him still enough to have a closer look at the problem. Gerhard made the quick decision to knock him out before he had the chance to start developing a full-scale "I hate the vets" neurotic complex, if it wasn't already too late to prevent it. A few hours later Gerhard phoned us, said he had found a small splinter, had flushed it out, and could we come and collect him ASAP since Dylan was registering his displeasure at the turn of events in his life by running through a repertoire of protest songs at full volume.

We went to fetch him and found him bandaged up and with instructions to take it easy for a week. A week! I was thinking more like a couple of days. Imagine the disruption an unexercised Dylan would make for that length of time. I'd have to build a soundproofed kennel in the backyard; at least the sound of hammering would drown him out.

Meanwhile, there was the one vaguely positive side effect—I could take Ollie on a trip down memory lane, back to one of our old stomping grounds where we had not been for some time, where there were rabbits, and where it was still unsafe to take Dylan. We traveled over to the university campus. It was a cool, gray evening and there was nobody much around, no playmates for Ollie, no individuals to pick fights with. It was lonely times like this that had led me to consider bringing a Dylan into our lives in the first place. We took a long walk, during which Ollie did nothing. The only animals I have ever seen put less effort into their exercise have been fifteen-year-old retrievers with arthritis. Other than lagging behind sniffing at plants for extended passages of time and sitting down in the middle of fields being existential, Ollie expended no energy whatsoever. "C'mon, boy, get a move on." This became my catchphrase. But now that I looked at him more carefully, I could see he was invoking a third method of time wasting: he was pausing to look back over his shoulder, and all around, and then to me. *Where is Dylan, Master?* This is what the look said. He had no one to beat up, no one to batter, no one whose behavior he could disapprove of and frown upon, no one to feel superior to, no one to guard and defend. He was missing his brother.

Back home he bounded into the house with unusual intent. Was Dylan still there? He went off to check this matter with some urgency. Once he had seen that all was well on that score, he turned on his heel and retired to his office to be aloof. Had he really been remotely concerned about the youngster's welfare? *As if.*

Using the stealthy teeth method, Dylan removed the bandage from his leg overnight. Mid-morning I took him for a test walk around the block to see how his recovery was going. He was right as rain, except that he kept looking over his shoulder, and then up to me. *Where is Ollie, Master?* the look seemed to say. That same evening—a twenty-four-hour convalescence was more than adequate—I took them out and let them free in a meadow. Dylan crouched low in the prone, "C'mon, let's do it, man!" pre-run position. Ollie ignored him.

"Ollie," I said, "you are a disgrace. This was *all* you wanted to do last night and it was *everything* you were missing."

Ollie looked at me. If a dog could wink, that's what he did. *Only kidding*, he seemed to say, before flying after his brother, who got out of his way just a second too late, or to put it another way, with perfect timing for all concerned.

Translating Dylan

We have often been stopped as Dylan has been getting down with his bad self. One day an Australian man pulled up, laughed, and scratched his head before asking Trezza: "What are we looking at here, then?" It's a fair question, the way his tail conformation works in conjunction with his front leg conformation while he travels by at thirty miles per hour and does his stuff:

Hello, pleased to meet you.

The basic tail, for perfect balance.

The deceptively aerodynamic ears.

The stealthy, dedicated hunter.

The kick-back and stretch (plus the Ollie
"What am I being now?").

A tale of two tails.

It's a hard-knock life.

Postscript: Leaving Ollie

In mid-September, I was walking Ollie and Dylan out at Winterton-on-Sea. Dylan had been misbehaving with the rabbits, as usual. Having finally got ahold of him, I had clipped him on to the leash, and we made our way back to the parking lot along the ridge of dune. It was a beautiful evening. Ollie, unusually, suddenly dived after a rabbit himself. He went up and down a couple of dunes at full speed. At this iniquitous turn of events, Dylan was rearing up on his back legs and bouncing, both to achieve a better view, and also because he was very cross. I let him go, to join in. I lost sight of him (of course), and of Ollie, too, but I heard some crying. *Oh shit,* I thought, *the rabbit's had it* (in the normal run of things, neither of them ever catches his prey). The crying became louder, and then I realized it was a noise I recognized: it was the sound of Ollie in distress.

He was still out of sight, but I found him in the dip of a dune, holding his leg up, at the first major joint above the foot, the high ankle, as I think of it, which is actually called the carpus. My first thought was that he must have twisted it, maybe even in a rabbit hole: it seems a miracle to me that they have both avoided an injury like this so far. I was in a bit of a spot, because Dylan was once more on the missing list. Ollie wouldn't move at all, so I carried him to a high dune, eventually found Dylan, and nursed Ollie back to the car, half-carrying, half-hopping along on three legs. Though Dylan is clearly missing his brother at the time of this writing, at that moment he appeared to have no canine empathy whatsoever: certainly he was no help, and apparently regarded Ollie's malingering as one of his usual prima donna acts.

X-rays were taken at the vet's office the following morning. Painkillers were given: perhaps it was tendon damage. Ollie was restricted to short exercise on his leash around the block. Our local vet "didn't like" the look of the X-rays, and so sent them to Ollie's specialist up in Fakenham. There was a set at the surgery there from when he had broken his leg a few years earlier, and our vet wanted a comparison.

On October 2, 2008, on the official publication date of *Fetching Dylan* in the United Kingdom (under the title *Along Came Dylan*), I was preparing to leave the house for a train to London to have dinner with my agent when I took a phone call from Lucas, the second in command at the local vet, who said, "No beating about the bush, it's bad news: Ollie almost certainly has osteosarcoma (cancer) in that bone, but we need to have him in to take samples for analysis, and to X-ray his lungs to see whether it has spread." Trezza was at work. For twenty minutes I thought I was okay, and then I started crying, and then I phoned my agent and canceled dinner. I went downstairs to stroke Ollie's head and to tell him not to have cancer.

The weeks that passed since were quite simply awful. Two bone samples were taken, neither of them with a positive result. His lungs were clear. I convinced myself that the vets were quacks and that all he had was a mild bone infection: Ollie is only six; he cannot die. *But*: his leg was not recovering, there was a lump there that was not going down, and though he was getting around the block without too much trouble, he was limping slightly by the end of these (relatively) short excursions (they took quite a long time because of all the "sit-down protests" from Ollie). On Halloween I took him up to Fakenham to see the specialist, who ran me through the various treatment options.

1. Keep up the painkillers until he shows signs of distress then take him to be (and this is the word that is used) *euthanized*. I prefer "put to sleep."

2. Chemotherapy. Meaning many trips to Cambridge sixty miles away and side effects that might include sickness and fur burns. This treatment really only offers pain relief, too, because what is happening—and here Gordon, the specialist, became dramatic and compelling in his description—is that "the main site is firing off clusters of *hundreds of thousands of cancerous cells* into the rest of Ollie."

3. Amputate. Could arrest progress for a while, perhaps up to a year. There was no way I was going to let Ollie be a three-legged dog. I have seen them

thrive, but not ones built on his supermodel lines, with a very high center of gravity, who also have cancer.

4. There's a treatment pioneered in the United States whereby the bone is taken out, irradiated, put back in, pinned, and plated. The technique is not at all widely available in the United Kingdom, and it comes with a great number of side effects such as infections and other complications. The specialist was skeptical about this way forward, but did not rule it out entirely.

There is a racecourse at Fakenham. After the consultation I went and sat in the parking lot there, pretending to read. It was gray and wet. To kill time I walked up past a couple of hurdles to the finishing post and back. One hour later I was looking at some new X-ray plates. The bone was deteriorating: where the line of the radius should have been sharp and white, it was nibbled at, like a mouse had been at it. But never mind that, the doctor said, "Look at this." He clipped a huge plate of Ollie's enormous lungs up onto the light box: there were more than a dozen tumors. Options 2, 3, and 4 were no longer options.

"How long has he got?" I asked.

"Six to eight weeks," he replied.

A couple of Sundays before he left us I took him up to Winterton-on-Sea to have one last look at the beach where he had unwittingly had his final run. There could have been no better spot for it than there, at least: Winterton was his favorite place on earth. One elderly lady came by with an elderly dog and remarked how beautiful Ollie was. It was dark, dusk, and cold, and he was wearing his fur-lined coat. The only part of him that was really visible was his head, but even under these circumstances his presence was remarkable. At moments like that over his last few weeks, as many fellow owners and other friends of Ollie said many kind words, we had it confirmed to us how everyone loved him, and we cried many tears. His final days were all organic chicken and sirloin steak; though, if the truth is told, that was his general lifestyle anyway. As I often used to tell him, he was a one-off in the dog world: the Special One. In certain lights and environments he didn't even look like a dog and was sometimes mistaken for a deer. You can't be more of a Special One than that.

Ollie was put to sleep on Monday, November 17, at

eleven o'clock. He is a huge absence around the place. As Trezza says, "I even miss his toxic breath."

He looked the picture of health as we took him into the operating room, still gleaming "like a giant mole," as Philip, who also advised me to hold him in my arms as it happened, continued to describe him. "You're going off to giant mole heaven, boy," he said, biting back his tears as he visited him one last time, on the preceding Sunday. Ollie had coughed a couple of times in the final few days, and had suddenly cried out from nowhere, as he sat on the sofa, and then held the leg up, all of which at least helped convince us that what lay ahead was the right course. It had to be done sooner rather than later, too, because the worst-case— and most likely—scenario was that he would break his leg, that it would simply crumble under him as he was walking around the block. We could not have that; we could not have our last memory being of him screaming out in pain.

As Gerhard, the chief vet at our local practice, the one who knows him best and who also loves him, I think, injected his leg with a lethal overdose of sedative, he was apologizing. "Sorry, Ollie," he was saying. "What am I doing to you, boy?" he was saying. Gerhard is a good man, with deep brown eyes set into a kind face. You could not ask for anyone better to carry out this task. Trezza was cradling Ollie's neck, whispering to him and crying onto his head. I had his body held against me, his huge, deep chest against my own. In my right hand I could feel his heart beating, too rapidly. As the fluid ran through his blood I felt the beat slow, and slow, and slow, until it stopped. He felt soft and warm in my arms, as if he were still alive, and his eyes remained slightly open, too. We laid him on the floor where Gerhard tested him for reflex: it was done, it was over. "You were very brave," he said to us. "Shall I leave you alone with him for a couple of minutes?" We nodded; we were not so brave that we could actually speak. He lay on the floor, looking as beautiful as he ever had. Trezza finally found her voice and told him that she loved him. I stroked his side and tickled his belly. Just before we left the room, I arranged his ears to look tidy.

We left the vet and drove away with tears streaming down our faces; back home in the kitchen we hugged, and Dylan got between us. He knew what must have happened, because he never does that. In the final few weeks I had often caught him licking Ollie's leg, trying to cure what could not be cured. At the moment he is a little lonely; he is used to being in a two-dog family. One day that situation will return. Ollie chanced across us, and in due course Dylan's new mate will appear. It is simply a matter of waiting for it to happen. Until then, we are looking after him, and he us.

Stephen Foster is the author of *Walking Ollie*, the account of his early days with his rescue dog, Ollie, which was a *Sunday Times* bestseller in the United Kingdom. Other works include the MacMillan PEN shortlisted story collection *It Cracks Like Breaking Skin*, the novels *Strides* and *Are You With Me?*, and *She Stood There Laughing*, his account of a season following Stoke City. He lives in Norwich, England, with his partner, Trezza, and Dylan.

For information on animal shelters, animal health, and ways you can support abused, abandoned, and forgotten pets, visit www.ASPCA .org, the website of the American Society for the Prevention of Cruelty to Animals.

Also Available from Stephen Foster

Before Dylan there was Ollie...

Here is the funny and charming story of how a growling, skittish man and his equally growling, skittish dog broke each other in, came to see eye to eye, and decided to become best friends.

T74.0109